Inequality in Capitalist Societies

Inequality is one of the most discussed topics of our time. Yet, we still do not know how to tackle the issue effectively. The book argues that this is due to the lack of understanding of the structures responsible for the persistence of social inequality. It inquires into the mechanisms that produce and reproduce invisible dividing lines in society. Based on original case studies of Brazil, Germany, India and Laos comprising thousands of interviews, the authors argue that invisible classes emerge in capitalist societies, both reproducing and transforming precapitalist hierarchies. At the same time, locally particular forms of inequality persist. Social inequality in the contemporary world has to be understood as a specific combination of precapitalist inequalities, capitalist transformation and a particular class structure that seems to emerge in all capitalist societies. The book links the configurations to an interpretation of global domination as well as to symbolic classification.

Surinder S. Jodhka is professor of Sociology at Jawaharlal Nehru University, New Delhi, and an affiliate Senior Fellow at the Centre de Sciences Humaines, New Delhi. He was visiting professor at various universities in Europe, North America and South Asia and is winner of the Amartya Sen Award. He specializes in inequality, caste and development and has published twelve books in these fields.

Boike Rehbein is professor for Society and Transformation in Asia and Africa at Humboldt University, Germany. He was visiting professor in Latin America, India, Laos, South Africa and Switzerland. He specializes in inequality, social theory and globalization and has published twenty-five books in these fields.

Jessé Souza is professor of Sociology at the Universidade Federal de Fluminense, Brazil. Previously, he was professor at various universities of Brazil and President of IPEA. He specializes on social theory and inequality and has published twenty-three books in these fields.

Routledge Studies in the Modern World Economy

Inequality in Capitalist Societies

Surinder S. Jodhka, Boike Rehbein
and Jessé Souza

Routledge
Taylor & Francis Group

LONDON AND NEW YORK

2017: 12551

First published 2018
by Routledge
2 Park Square, Milton Park, Abingdon, Oxon OX14 4RN

and by Routledge
711 Third Avenue, New York, NY 10017

Routledge is an imprint of the Taylor & Francis Group, an informa business

© 2018 Surinder S. Jodhka, Boike Rehbein and Jessé Souza

The right of Surinder S. Jodhka, Boike Rehbein and Jessé Souza
to be identified as authors of this work has been asserted by them
in accordance with sections 77 and 78 of the Copyright, Designs
and Patents Act 1988.

British Library Cataloguing-in-Publication Data
A catalogue record for this book is available from the British Library

Library of Congress Cataloging-in-Publication Data
Names: Jodhka, Surinder S., author | Rehbein, Boike, author. |
 Souza, Jessé, author.
Title: Inequality in capitalist societies / by Surinder S. Jodhka,
 Boike Rehbein and Jessé Souza.
Description: Abingdon, Oxon ; New York, NY : Routledge, 2018. |
 Series: Routledge studies in the modern world economy ; 168 |
 Includes bibliographical references and index.
Identifiers: LCCN 2017004151 | ISBN 9781138683754 (hardback) |
 ISBN 9781315544366 (ebook)
Subjects: LCSH: Equality. | Equality—Economic aspects. |
 Capitalism—Social aspects.
Classification: LCC HM821 .J63 2018 | DDC 306.3—dc23
LC record available at https://lccn.loc.gov/2017004151

ISBN: 978-1-138-68375-4 (hbk)
ISBN: 978-1-315-54436-6 (ebk)

Typeset in Galliard
by Apex CoVantage, LLC

MIX
Paper from
responsible sources
FSC
www.fsc.org   FSC® C013604   Printed and bound by CPI Group (UK) Ltd, Croydon, CR0 4YY

11. 12. 2017 | € 119,34

Contents

Figures

Tables

Introduction

In his deservedly acclaimed and widely read book, *Capital in the Twenty-First Century* (2014), Thomas Piketty argues that inequality has been increasing on a global scale from the 1970s until today. According to him, since the 1970s capital returns have surpassed economic growth, which privileges inherited capital over salaries. In the preceding period, wars and political interventions had gradually reduced inequality until reaching the highest level of equality around 1950. Piketty adds that his book explains the phenomenon from the perspective of economics. He regrets that it uncovers only part of the story as it does not include the social structures beneath economic inequality. We agree: most research on inequality focuses on economic indicators but does not explain who is rich and who is poor and why this is the case.

The present book seeks to contribute to this explanation. It agrees with Piketty's diagnosis of global economic inequality and with his call for a better sociological understanding of it. We claim that this lack of understanding is not a coincidence but part of an agenda – partly conscious, partly subconscious – to make the structures and mechanisms producing inequality invisible. Inequality has become an industry in itself with thousands of highly paid experts managing the problem in international organizations, think tanks, government bodies, NGOs and universities. The emphasis is on the management of inequality, not on a serious struggle against it. The result is a host of data, which fills any brain with numbers and graphs and little understanding of the subject. Such data is sometimes used for isolated political interventions.

A couple of years ago, we witnessed the speech by a senior official of one such agency, who claimed to have solved the problem of defining the middle class – based on ownership of a car. Because the speech was given in Vietnam, a Vietnamese in the audience stood up after the lecture and pointed to the fact that he would not buy a car due to congestion of the streets in Ho Chi Minh City and therefore traveled by motorcycle. He asked whether he did not belong to the middle class even though he owned a consulting firm. The senior officer, who had traveled business class just to deliver this talk, replied, "Oh, maybe my theory is wrong." This casual approach to inequality demonstrates the disinterest in solving the problem of inequality and in the actual suffering of billions of people it affects. Inequality is a game, a riddle at best – and not the reason why half of the world population lives in poverty and humiliation and why almost the entire remainder has to labor in order to finance the dominant class, which comprises less than 0.1 percent of the world population.

In the first chapter of this book, we argue that the inability to understand social inequality has intellectual reasons as well. It has been impossible to resolve the problem because many assumptions inherited from the European Enlightenment have not been called into question. These assumptions include the interpretation of history as an evolution toward a superior model of society embodied by European and North American nation-states, the concept of democracy as a community of free, equal and individualized citizens and the notion of capitalism as defined by competition for capital. We try to show that these assumptions contribute to the resilience of inequality and need to be overcome.

Most assessments of inequality regard it as an outcome of competition between equal individuals for economic goods and money. This view entails that inequality can be alleviated by improving the rules of competition and/or by redistributing economic entities, especially money. Indeed, we experience ourselves as free individuals who determine our own life-courses and may (or may not) be successful in the pursuit of our goals. In this book, we wish to demonstrate that before any action in society, before any competition and even before our first steps as babies, we are shaped and limited by social structures, which we study in some detail.

Key terms

The following chapters combine case studies of Brazil, Germany, India and Laos with a comparison and brief analysis of global inequality. They focus on *social inequality* and argue that the roots of any type of inequality lie in domination. Social inequality is not only determined by the distribution of economic goods and money but also by the distribution of other forms of *capital* and *habitus* as well as by the historical development of society and by *symbolic classification*. We use the terms capital and habitus following Pierre Bourdieu (1984): capital comprises all valuable resources that are necessary to perform competitive actions in society, whereas habitus refers to the embodied patterns of action that are intelligible and acceptable. Social inequality, in this book, signifies the differential access to activities and goods that are valued in society. Our research shows that the disposal of capital is not so much a result of social action but – similar to what Piketty has shown with regard to economic wealth – a heritage that is reproduced from one generation to the next.

Contrary to our initial hypothesis, we discovered that this legacy is passed on within class boundaries. We define *class* as a tradition with a common culture that reproduces itself from one generation to the next by passing on relevant capital and symbolically distinguishing itself from other classes. This concept can be operationalized by establishing the limits of social mobility. However, class only explains inequality in nation-states with a long capitalist past. In other societies, many precapitalist structures of inequality persist that have to be interpreted within the particular framework of history, culture and social configuration. We will offer a means of interpretation under the heading of *socioculture*.

Our analyses show that the structures of inequality in a capitalist nation-state can be explained as a combination of sociocultures and class order. The capitalist classes, however, emerge from precapitalist hierarchies as well. As relational categories, classes cannot be understood merely on the basis of capital but have to be viewed from the perspective of social practice as well. Practices are not created spontaneously but are passed on through training from one generation to the next. We demonstrate in the chapters of this book that this training largely takes place within the limits of class. Thus, the dividing lines between the classes as well as class cultures are reproduced from one generation to the next and they comprise practices and ideas that are rooted in earlier and often precapitalist times.

The book seeks to explore how sociocultures and the capitalist transformation combine to form structures of inequality in different nation-states. It also compares these structures in order to find similarities and differences and to draw more general theoretical conclusions. Societies and nation-states have different histories, precapitalist structures and therefore different sociocultures. This also means that they differ in their configurations of inequality. The most important factor of the differences between the nation-states in the global South is the role of colonialism, whereas the most important factor in Northatlantic societies seems to be the ways in which "universal" citizenship was established.[1]

The final chapter will compare the four case studies and link them to the problem of global inequality and to the order of nation-states. Both, in turn, are partly explained by the relation of Northatlantic societies to the global South and its roots in colonialism. We argue that capitalism is a particular regime of domination not only within nation-states but on a global scale. Therefore, the final chapter also explores the global extent of this particular type of domination and its relation to the classes.

The four nation-states we study comprise four or five classes and varying degrees of persisting precapitalist inequalities. It seems that a four-class structure based on solid dividing lines is emerging in most states. At the same time, earlier sociocultures persist and inform the actual configuration of the classes. We have found that the dividing lines between the classes become more rigid with time and that the marginalized classes are larger in countries with a strong and unequal colonial heritage. The dividing lines are constituted and reproduced by symbolic classification, which confers different moral values to classes of people. Our empirical research inspired us to distinguish the dividing lines of dignity, expressivity and aloofness. They will be addressed in each chapter, but especially in Chapter 4.

Each social class has a culture, which predisposes its members for specific institutions, institutional segments and functions in the division of work. We use the term *division of work* as a more comprehensive concept than the division of labor because we look at the distribution of all socially relevant activities and not just formal wage-labor. Selection for the division of work based on symbolic classification reproduces the structures of inequality. The persons selecting members of elite clubs or CEOs are likely to be members of the highest class and/or to apply its selection criteria. Even if the selection process is entirely transparent and rational, the selecting persons will apply the most exclusive criteria for the most exclusive jobs and these criteria will be embodied by the members of the most exclusive class, as they were socialized in the corresponding social environment. In capitalist societies, the best carry out the most important functions in the division of work. This seems to be based on merit but is actually based on class.

The circular production and reproduction of class via inheritance of capital and cultural patterns, active and passive symbolic classification, selection and actual practice is made invisible by the focus on economic indicators and by the interpretation of inequality as a result of meritocratic competition between equal individuals. This perspective on inequality contributes to its reproduction. Therefore, this book seeks to offer a perspective that makes possible an actual combat against inequality.

Data and methodology

On the basis of empirical research in four world regions, we have developed a new approach to the understanding of inequality. We compare four nation-states that are very different in size, culture, history, economic indicators and "modernization", namely Brazil, Germany, India and Laos. We have conducted research on inequality in each of these countries for at least a decade and draw on a total of about three thousand qualitative interviews. For this book, we have conducted open life-course interviews using the same questionnaire in each country, with slight variations due to the different cultural environments. We use 108 interviews from Brazil, 61 from Germany, 80 from India and 74 from Laos that are more or less representative of age, gender, region, educational background and income. All interviews were conducted in the vernacular languages and interpreted by multicultural groups including many locals. On the basis of our preliminary results, we added representative questionnaire surveys comprising 2,970 cases in Germany, 610 in Brazil and 648 in Laos. All statistical information in this book is based on our interviews and surveys. We are not using any secondary data sources.

The life-course interview comprised questions in six categories: family background, childhood, education, leisure time and/or professional life, social life and perspectives for the future. The respondents were only interrupted if vital information was missing from their discourse. Family background questions were supposed to elucidate the issue of heritage over at least three generations. The questions on childhood and education were aimed at social environment, parenting style and the formation of primary habitus, which is the foundation of the habitus, as opposed to later modifications and amendments that we subsume under the term *secondary habitus*. The questions on leisure and work sought information about the core of social position. Social life questions amended this information and added social capital. Questions regarding assessment of one's own future elicited a lot about the respondent's view of his or her social position and classification. Several questions on classification and social data complemented the questionnaire.

All interviews were transcribed and interpreted in sequence analysis. The goal was to first determine relevant forms of capital and habitus traits and to then distinguish types. Research on inequality is often limited to isolated items. But social inequality and especially class become intelligible only through an analysis of the combination of items. Each factor reinforces the others but remains a merely statistical item in itself if we do not study the relation of all factors to one another. For this reason, it would be theoretically wrong and empirically unsatisfactory to define or measure class on the basis of one factor, such as economic capital or educational degree. Even though the correlations between class membership and these two factors are very strong, they remain statistical.

Therefore, we analyze the combination of characteristics. Only certain combinations of factors occur in reality, while others are rare. A peasant from Laos or a marginalized person in Brazil do not attend the opera. Furthermore, we tried to understand the entirety of the possible combinations in order to explain their reproduction. Finally, we studied the entire life-course, together with that of the respondents' ancestors. A CEO may become unemployed and a football player may become rich – but if this happens at all, it is usually only for a limited period of time and only true for this particular individual in the family.

We looked for a theoretical concept to grasp the varying combination of changing characteristics and found it in Ludwig Wittgenstein's *family resemblance* (Wittgenstein 1984: aphorism 65). Wittgenstein illustrates this combination with regard to a human family: all members of a family have some things in common but no two members share exactly the same traits. "Different similarities between the members of a family overlap and crisscross: stature, face, eye color, walk, temper" (aphorism 67; our translation). Many family members share the same stature and some of them also share the eye color, but do not have the same facial traits, which they share with other family members. "We see a complex web of similarities that overlap and crisscross each other. Small and big similarities." (aphorism 66; our translation) It is impossible to reduce the characteristics to general categories. One family member's stature was altered by his profession, another's nose through a punch and yet another's emotions by a hormonal disorder. There is no overarching explanation for all of these.

We applied the concept of family resemblance to our dataset. In order to find the existing combinations and the social "families", the combination of relevant factors had to be analyzed properly. We determined the forms of capital and habitus traits that were most important in the life-courses of our respondents. In terms of background, social origin (cultural and economic capital of the family), parenting styles and social environment of the family turned out to be the most relevant traits. We operationalized economic capital as income and items and money possessed, cultural capital as level and type of education, social capital as circle of friends, memberships and social environment, and symbolic capital as family name and respect from the community. Finally, we added those aspects of the habitus which our interviews revealed as significant and unequally distributed: self-confidence, discipline, an active attitude to life, goal-orientation, work ethos and optimism. All characteristics vary between the nation-states we studied and have to be modified accordingly. The combination of all factors also varies from individual to individual but presents a certain configuration of family resemblances for each class. The corresponding characteristics are passed on within the class from one generation to the next.

Because Bourdieu never operationalized the concept of habitus, we had to develop a method of analysis. We started with "habitus hermeneutics" (Lange-Vester and Teiwes-Kügler 2013), which was elaborated on the basis of Bourdieu's theory. It is a sophisticated attempt to operationalize the concept on the basis of qualitative interviews. The method uses material from everyday practice but also life-course interviews, determines "elementary categories", which characterize habitus, and finally constructs ideal-types. The categories are defined as binary oppositions and developed inductively. Both the categories and their application to particular cases result from interpretive work with semi-structured life-course interviews. The interpretation focuses at least to the same degree on the manner of how things are said, as to their content. The hypothesis of habitus hermeneutics is that characteristics of the habitus appear in the social practice of replying to interview questions.

The procedure, which we developed in the course of our research in Germany, slightly deviates from habitus hermeneutics in a couple of ways. First, we claim that the interview also delivers information and not only expresses a habitus. Therefore, we also asked questions aiming at information about the life-course. Second, over the years and based on hundreds of case studies, we established a list of questions and items that are relevant in terms of capital and habitus. Finally, we paid as much attention to capital as to the habitus. While habitus hermeneutics only aims at the construction of habitus types, we also try to construct classes including the division of capital.

We came up with an encoding matrix for the habitus, which is composed of four dimensions. Some categories were conceived of as binary oppositions in the sense of habitus hermeneutics, and some as tendencies. The oppositions point to synchronic traits and the tendencies to diachronic orientations. In the third dimension, we correlated the tendencies with the available information on grandparents, parents and parenting style in order to determine the options for social mobility. Finally, we looked at contradictions and contingencies as very few habitus are entirely coherent and ideal-typical (Lahire 1998).

Initially, we applied the same approach to our study of Laos, India and Brazil. In the course of our research, we realized that the habitus categories have to be adapted to the sociocultural context. This implies that we put a strong emphasis on inductive interview interpretation, which we combined with the critique of our initial categories. We also added questionnaire surveys on the basis of our qualitative interpretations. Both types of datasets were subjected to a multiple correspondence analysis (MCA), which fits the theoretical notion of family resemblance. This procedure will be explained in the second chapter.[2]

Structure of the book

Chapters 2 to 5 present the empirical results of our research. The theoretical foundations are discussed in the first chapter while the theoretical and empirical conclusions are drawn by the last chapter and linked to the global scope of capitalism and domination. The conclusion summarizes the results and sketches their political relevance. Each chapter can be read for itself but each case study is conceived of in such a way that it focuses on a different aspect of social inequality. Chapter 2 focuses on class, Chapter 3 on sociocultures, Chapter 4 on dividing lines and Chapter 5 on symbolic classification and intersections of inequality. Only in combination do the four chapters make sense of social inequality.

Chapter 1, outlining our theoretical approach, aims at clarifying the concepts we use and their relation to mainstream research on inequality. We argue that a new approach (including new concepts) is necessary because the focus on economics and capitalism obscures the structures of inequality. In order to access these structures, we need a conceptual apparatus which is abstract enough to be applied to different types of society and concrete enough to make sense of everyday life as it is experienced by us all.

The first case study, presented in the second chapter, deals with Germany. It gives an outline of the country's class structure, which has developed over centuries. The degree and the mode of reproduction of this structure are addressed rather briefly. More attention is given to the habitus types in German society and their everyday relevance. We also devote some space to the discussion of migration to Germany and its relation to inequality. Finally, the intersection of class and gender is addressed.

Chapter 3 about Laos focuses on the emergence of classes out of earlier sociocultures as well as the persistence and transformation of the sociocultures. Both the capitalist class structure and the configuration of sociocultures are demonstrated empirically. The chapter also introduces the habitus types we found in Laos and compares them to the German scenario. The same is done with regard to gender inequality.

Habitus and gender are not addressed extensively by the remaining chapters. Chapters 4 and 5 rather focus on the symbolic production and reproduction of inequality. The fourth chapter studies Brazil. It first introduces the classes of Brazil and briefly characterizes them and their origins in precapitalist sociocultures. The bulk of the chapter is devoted to the invisible lines between the classes, their reproduction and their moral significance in all spheres of life, including the current political struggle in the country.

Chapter 5 deals with India. It is mainly about the notion of caste and its relevance for understanding inequality both in India and in the rest of the world. We try to show that caste loses some of its relevance in favor of class but continues to persist. Caste also demonstrates how inequality works in everyday life. Far from being an exotic Indian peculiarity, it can be considered to be the epitome of social inequality.

The final chapter consists of three parts. The first compares the four case studies in order to establish general characteristics of inequality in capitalist societies and to identify and understand particularities of each country or type of country. The second part of the chapter seeks to theorize the general functioning of social inequality in capitalist societies and beyond. In the third part, we anchor the national structures of inequality in the global context of domination and capitalism. This part is somewhat speculative and calls for a more thorough study, which we hope to deliver in the near future.

Notes

1   We will refer to the countries of Western Europe, the US and Canada as Northatlantic societies, while we call the former "Third World" the global South.
2   Joint research in Brazil and Germany was funded by Alexander von Humboldt-Stiftung. We wish to thank the foundation for this.

1 Understanding social inequality

This chapter introduces the core concepts and the general approach of the following chapters. This is necessary since we cannot draw on an existing theory of inequality. All major theories of inequality have been constructed on the basis of Northatlantic societies or have remained restricted to the case of one nation-state. As we propose to compare four radically different societies, we need a theoretical framework that can be applied to the four cases without losing all of its explanatory power.

Our research showed social class to be much more relevant for the understanding of inequality than is assumed by most studies of contemporary societies. In order to study social class, we draw on Pierre Bourdieu's notions of capital and habitus. These notions are more relevant for the study of a country with a long capitalist past, such as Germany, than for the study of Laos and India. In these cases, precapitalist structures are at least as relevant for contemporary inequality. We deal with them under the heading of socioculture. Finally, we argue that the symbolic dimension of inequality has been underestimated by most research on the topic. In terms of production and of legitimation of inequality, symbolic classification of groups of people plays a key role.

This chapter first offers a brief critique of the mainstream perspective on inequality. Then, it turns to the neglected historical and symbolic dimensions in the study of inequality. The remainder of the chapter is devoted to the construction of a framework integrating the notions of class, socioculture and symbolic classification. The notion of class is introduced with reference to Bourdieu's concepts of capital and habitus and then expanded to meet the criteria generated by our empirical research.

The conventional view of inequality

In academia and everyday life, we tend to think of society in the Western liberal tradition. According to this view, which we call *symbolic liberalism*, society consists of formally and naturally equal individuals, inequality results from regulated competition between them and any type of privilege is therefore based on individual merit. This means that inequality between the individuals supposedly results from differences in achievement. As the individuals are regarded as biologically equal and socially endowed with equal rights at birth, symbolic liberalism supposes them to have the same opportunities. This is the main assumption of symbolic liberalism from Hobbes (1968) to Locke (1967) to Friedman (1962). It also informs the constitution of most democracies. Whoever is poor or humiliated has to bear at least part of the blame. Whoever is rich or respected has achieved something as an individual.

This view of inequality is corroborated by everyday observations. Even if we deny that we are all equal from birth and before the law, we seem to be individuals who have to come to terms with reality and find our own way through the social world as individuals. We are individualized, disciplined to perform a particular, increasingly individualized function in the division of labor. In this function, we contribute to the "wealth of nations" (Smith 1998). Each job and each remuneration is subject to competition between several individuals. This competition results in inequality: some win and some lose. There are rich proletarians and poor aristocrats, anyone can win the lottery and a talented, ambitious and smart person can become a football player, an actress or an entrepreneur. All of us can think of examples proving this point and thereby supporting symbolic liberalism.

In this book, we argue that social inequality is not a result of competition but a consequence of structures that have their roots in precapitalist society. Theories of social inequality as well as the political discourse and common sense have assumed that the transformation of society toward capitalism produces a complete rupture with the past. Right with the transformation, the population was supposed to be individualized into free and equal citizens, either instantaneously on the basis of a constitution or in a process of reform and revolution. This presumably brings about a shift from a closed system of inequality and hierarchies to an open system of differential rewards based on individual achievement, ability and distinction. According to this view, inequality results from engagement in a market, which is about the increase of capital. Supposedly, capitalism is the highest form of the evolution of society, either absolutely or until being replaced by a more equal society, and is embodied in Northatlantic societies. Liberal and Marxist interpretations merely disagree in their assessment of the unequal distribution of capital.

From this perspective, one cannot see that inequality in capitalist societies is a continuation of earlier structures of inequality. Early symbolic liberalism and the first capitalist democracies considered only the citizens to be free and equal, while the majority of social groups (such as slaves, women, nonwhites and laborers) were excluded from the community of citizens and therefore unequal. The lower ranks of precapitalist society as well as colonized peoples were excluded from capitalist society. When these groups were included into the community of equals and accepted as citizens, they remained underprivileged and unequal, because they always had to start from a less favorable position as latecomers.

What is more relevant to our argument is that these groups have never been able to acquire the symbolic characteristics of equal citizens. Up to this day, there is a distrust regarding blacks, women, lower classes or people from the global South taking important positions in society. They simply do not have what it takes, in terms of symbolic classification and in terms of habitus, because they have inherited less valuable social traits. Even under conditions of complete equality of opportunities, these groups would not compete on a level playing field as they retain negative symbolic characteristics on the basis of earlier historical inequalities.

Symbolic inequality

While the game of competition rules the visible world, privileges are passed on from generation to generation invisibly. These privileges include not only all kinds of capital but also the symbolic distinctions between social groups and their evaluation. All groups share the symbolic universe of capitalism characterized by meritocracy and the hierarchy of social classification, which makes some classes virtuous on the basis of their inherited symbolic characteristics, which we will discuss in more detail in the following chapters. Those groups who do not inherit a sufficient degree of the valued social characteristics are regarded as inferior and will never compete on a level playing field.

The symbolic inequality between the classes has to be expressed in a manner that makes it appear natural instead of socially constructed and socially inherited. Otherwise, it would not be legitimate. This is the purpose of symbolic liberalism and the meritocratic myth. It is specific for contemporary capitalist societies that inequality is at once naturalized and invisibilized. According to symbolic liberalism, inequality results from the competition of equal individuals on free but legally regulated markets. As success on these markets is supposed to be the outcome of merit but actually reflects the order of domination, it includes both a legitimation of social inequality and an expression of class structure. It includes a declassation and humiliation of entire groups of human beings – namely the lower classes, the global South and other groups – who are perceived to be at once less virtuous and less successful. We refer to this declassation as *symbolic racism*.

The relevance of symbolic evaluations and dividing lines in society has not been acknowledged properly by mainstream theories of inequality. This is partly due to the focus on the economy. If inequality is only about the distribution of economic entities, especially money, the symbolic dimension becomes rather irrelevant. However, the disregard for the symbolic dimension has deeper philosophical roots. It is partly based on the dichotomy of mind and body established by Descartes and picked up by Hobbes, Locke and Smith. Against this background, the study of society has become a quest for eternal laws governing the movement of social entities. This quest is even reflected in Marxism.

We reject the distinctions between being and consciousness, mind and body, economy and ideology and functional system and life-world. Instead, we interpret society entirely as *meaningful practice*. From this perspective, the symbolic mediation of power is the structural root of inequality. This is domination. Power is understood as the impersonal possibility of influencing the social definition and practice of life. Symbol is understood as comprising all perceivable forms of meaning (Cassirer 1997), from signs to art to language. We argue that human practice is always symbolically mediated and that the understanding of this process is the key to understanding society. Inequality is about domination, not about money or business. Even capitalism has to be understood as a symbolically mediated practice. We agree with those interpretations of capitalism that regard it as a largely unconscious practice but we deny that it is "material" or guided by natural laws. It is not even about material things but about symbolically mediated things. Machines, capital, money, exchange value and labor are all something completely different without symbolic mediation. Socially, they would be nothing in this case. A bank note that is not recognized as money is a sheet of paper and a stock exchange that is not understood in its meaning ceases to exist.

The core of our approach consists in the integration of the symbolic universe into the study of social structures, capitalism and the distribution of capital, labor, privileges and power. Later in this chapter and extensively in Chapters 4 and 5, we will demonstrate the relevance of the symbolic dimension for the study of inequality. We argue that without classification, symbolic racism, invisible dividing lines and legitimation, social inequality would not be possible – especially once material goods have been redistributed. We will also show how these symbolic inequalities are continuations and transformations of precapitalist hierarchies. Therefore, a historical and comparative perspective is absolutely necessary to understand social inequality.

Capitalist transformation

Social structures, cultures and practices are subject to constant changes and sometimes even revolutions. New institutions appear, old ones are done away with, new discourses emerge, economic crises erupt or oil is discovered. Some of these changes are so radical that they produce a new configuration and a new social hierarchy. We refer to these radical changes as *transformations*. Transformations are closely related to revolutions but often do not occur in the wake of a revolution. Wars, changes in the social organization and political interventions seem to be more frequent cases of transformations than revolutions. Even though these changes are radical, they are only transformations and not new creations because they build on earlier structures. Social structures are relatively persistent. Aristocracy or working class, the value of a PhD or the reputation of a doctor do not disappear overnight. They lose part of their value or are reassessed in a new framework but they are not simply done away with. This is true for the entire system of structures, cultures and practices. We refer to these systems as *sociocultures*. Any contemporary practice has a long history, which it partly incorporates. Its current form blends transformed and persisting elements with new elements. This is true for society at large as well. We can think of society as a mountain consisting of layers of rocks and sediment.

It is important to acknowledge the continuities in spite of the radical nature of capitalist transformation. First, capitalist transformation only modified precapitalist structures but does not erase them. Second, precapitalist inequalities persisted because of the unequal integration of precapitalist ranks. The same process took place in Europe and the Americas. At first, capitalist society only comprised a few privileged groups and successively integrated the entire population, mainly due to protests and revolutions. Capitalism does bring about a social and economic transformation through differentiation. New occupations and social categories (such as middle class) come into being, but this does not necessarily do away with older standards of evaluation. The old and new coexist, and often reinforce each other. The excluded groups are integrated unequally but in the symbolic universe, all citizens are equal because they have the same rights. Even though socioeconomic mobility is minimal in Northatlantic societies (cf. Chapter 2), the few cases of stars or entrepreneurs coming from unequally integrated groups serve as examples to sustain symbolic liberalism.

In many former colonies of Asia and Africa, however, the entire population was declared equal citizens upon gaining independence. The preceding structures of inequality were immediately transformed into capitalist classes. Linked to revolutionary struggles, there was more socioeconomic mobility in the newly independent states than would have been possible at any moment in the history of Northatlantic societies. At the same time, persisting inequalities were rendered invisible much faster because underprivileged groups were formally equal right from the start and were open to some socioeconomic mobility. This process still continues in parts of the global South.

The transformation does not significantly reshuffle the conditions for participating in capitalism and democracy. The distribution of resources has remained the same. A few revolutionaries and a couple of entrepreneurs have moved up into the ruling class but in general, the peasants have remained poor, uneducated, peripheral, despised and powerless while the aristocrats have kept their castles and their prestige. Formally, these structures have been abolished in almost all capitalist societies. This made their reproduction even more efficient because they are invisible and, within the symbolic universe, even inexistent.

Along with the specific relation between symbolic universe and social structures, capitalism creates a few novelties which are relevant to the understanding of inequality. These novelties have transformed society. With the capitalist transformation, the social position is no longer equivalent to the type of activities one performs. Social structure and division of labor become detached from each other, while the population seems to be transformed into a mass of equal and disciplined individuals. The focus on the division of labor makes society more productive. We can observe the commodification of everything in a country like Laos in real time. Land, human bodies, water, the products of nature are commodified and used as means of production. People are trained in workshops organized by international organizations to behave like economic agents in competitive markets (see Rehbein 2007). Then, they are trained to develop capabilities that are competitive in the labor market. All of this is entirely new to the majority of the rural population – and to any precapitalist society.

Another novelty introduced by capitalism is that political order, division of labor and virtually every capitalist society is based on science. Before capitalism, there has neither been a scientific legitimation of political order nor a scientific organization of the division of labor. This is something one can witness presently emerging in Laos as well. Of course, the European development of science and its link to capitalism are well known. We are also aware of the role of science in the legitimation of social action, from laws to political measures to investment decisions. This is entirely unknown to a noncapitalist society.

The capitalist transformation certainly first took place in Europe, even if Europe's rise had to rely on the existing world-system dominated by Asia with its relatively more developed industry and trade (Abu-Lughod 1989) and in connection with colonialism (Frank 1998). Most of the apparent novelties that European capitalism created had existed before in Asia, often in a more "developed" form (Hobson 2004). However, symbolic liberalism as the dominant symbolic universe is a European creation as well as the link between an increasing division of labor and science.

The capitalist transformation creates a similar surface everywhere but meets different historical conditions and takes place in different historical processes and periods. Histories, precapitalist structures and therefore sociocultures vary between societies and nation states. This also means that they differ in their configurations of inequality (Rehbein 2011). The most important factor is the role of colonialism. In this regard, we can distinguish between three types of capitalist states. The states in which a bourgeois revolution introduced capitalism and democracy have transformed precapitalist structures by successively integrating the lower ranks. In contrast, some of the former colonies were dominated by descendants of the former colonizers who formed the ruling classes of the now independent states, especially in the Americas. The native peoples were partly killed and partly integrated as lower classes along with the former slaves. The third type are former colonies that transformed the precolonial and colonial structures directly into unequal democracies, especially in Asia.

The prehistory of a capitalist nation-state makes a difference to its structural inequality, as we will demonstrate in the subsequent chapters. The most important differences are the relation to colonialism and the integration of previously underprivileged groups into the nation-state. However, the particular types of precapitalist hierarchies also matter, as they persist underneath the capitalist surface. Nevertheless, it is necessary to understand the capitalist surface as well. For this purpose, we draw on Pierre Bourdieu's theory of inequality.

Habitus and capital

The core concept of Bourdieu's sociology is that of *habitus*. The concept is based on the assumption that a human being has the tendency to act in the way in which he or she has learned to act (Bourdieu 1990). It is a kind of psychosomatic memory. Behavior from prior interactions is put to use again once a similar situation arises. In a mostly stable environment, a common practice is acquired and is then incorporated as an enduring and stable pattern. With learning, one adopts a pattern which can be applied in a corresponding situation. Through multiple repetitions, the pattern becomes imprinted on the person; this pattern becomes habitualized. That implies a standardization with regards to scenarios of use and a somatization of segments of actions. Bourdieu referred to these internalized schemata as *dispositions*. He emphasized the unconscious character of dispositions, because these dispositions are always somaticized.

In this regard, Bourdieu's argument follows that of Maurice Merleau-Ponty (1964). According to Merleau-Ponty, we do not have a body; rather, we *are* a body. We do not see with an eye; rather, we are among things in a seeing way. We do not control the hand; rather, the hand has its own somatized memory and practice. As humans, we are bodies which move in the world, and this practical world is concrete, meaningful and socialized. Social organization is really an organization of the body and its conduct (Bourdieu 1990), and it is expressed, for example, in a prideful person's upright gait and in the cowering of the dominated. The social world imprints a proper and correct program, a character in the truest sense of the word, on a body, just as how a message is engraved with a pen on a writing tablet. Similar to a writing tablet, the body is also a kind of mnemonic device – both for the actor and for the observer. Bourdieu develops this argument like Merleau-Ponty: what the body learns, one does not possess but that is what one is.

According to Bourdieu, all of the activities a person performs are similar to one another. The habitus establishes something like a style (Bourdieu 1984). At the same time, behavior represents a structuring of existence, an element of a life-form and a social resource. Because social structures are imprinted on the habitus, it tends to reproduce these structures, especially in those cases where the present social environment and the conditions from which the habitus arose are identical. If one grew up in "small town USA" and continues to live there, most patterns of action would be perfectly adapted to the environment in spite of all the changes on a national and global scale. The habitus organizes practices in such a way that they tend to reproduce those conditions from which the habitus emerged. On the basis of the habitus, actions are neither spontaneous nor predetermined; rather, they are the result of a necessary connection between disposition and objective environment (Swartz 1997). Both are based on similar and sometimes identical social structures. The habitus not only tends to reproduce earlier behavior but instead *seeks* conditions which correspond to its generation – mainly because it is shaped for these conditions. The explanation of an action is a reconstruction of the precise correlation between the conditions under which a habitus was formed, and the conditions of its application. This means that the application can change the social structures but only if the habitus does not fully coincide with them.

The conditions for the generation and application of a habitus are in many ways not singular but are instead valid for various people, groups and classes.

The conditions are at least to a certain extent homogeneous in a particular social environment. Within a group, homologous conditions prevail; therefore, habitus are also homologous. Against this background, Bourdieu attempted to deduce the behavior of a social group from its social conditions of existence. In his most famous book, *Distinction* (1984), he argued that even the very subjective taste – for food, art and even manners – was rooted in the habitus and could thereby be explained by the study of the conditions of existence of a social group.

This line of argument presupposes a unity of the habitus and a relative homogeneity of the conditions of its application. The presuppositions only apply if a person acts the same way in the same situations and only if all members of the social group have a similar life-course. Both presuppositions are dubious. The human is fragmented, inconsistent and diverse (Lahire 1998). Regarding the human as a homogeneous entity with a singular identity is a curious and unfortunately well-established tradition, and this tradition corresponds neither to reality nor to a norm. Apart from this, the social reality constantly changes and is very complex. This is reflected in the fact that the correlations between social conditions and specific aspects of taste presented by Bourdieu (1984) are not very strong statistically.

In his later work, Bourdieu acknowledged the diversity of social practice and limited his analyses to particular realms of the social world, which he called "fields". He developed this concept partly with regard to Weber's sociology of religion and partly on the basis of Ludwig Wittgenstein's notion of language game (Bourdieu and Wacquant 1992). In his *Philosophical Investigations* (1984), Wittgenstein tried to show that there is not one uniform language that is used in exactly the same way in every instance but that there are many different possible uses of language that depend on the purpose and the context. He called a recurring context a *language game*. Each game has its own rules and goals. Wittgenstein argued that this is true for language use as well. It varies according to context and there are "countless" contexts but they are not random. Just like games, they have a certain stability and regularity (1984: aphorism 207). This stability is linked to the fact that contexts do not emerge spontaneously but are socially regulated and to a certain degree standardized. "The word 'language game' serves to emphasize that language use is part of an activity or a form of life." (1984: 23) Whoever learns to play a language game needs to learn a form of practice and a set of norms. Just like Austin and Bourdieu, Wittgenstein insisted that this process needs not be conscious (202).

A language game has a regularity and stability because its participants have incorporated the ways of playing it. The use of language in an utterance resembles a move in a game. However, there is not one basic structure of a game in general. Chess has little in common with volleyball or hide-and-seek. The goal of the game can vary as well as the number of players, the types of action and the rules. Wittgenstein argued that this applies to language as well. He listed such diverse types of language use as saying thank you, asking, ordering, praying, describing, guessing, playing theatre, telling a joke and translating (1984: 23).

Each has a different context and is linked to a different set of practices. Wittgenstein called the set of practices including language use a *form of life* (19). The form of life cannot be clearly delimited or reduced to a basic type.

This also means that the goals and the required abilities differ in each form of life. It is not guaranteed that the same habitus has the same "value" in each form of life and that it plays out the same way in each form of life. However, according to Wittgenstein, it is likely that it works the same way at different times in the same form of life. This claim is implied in Bourdieu's concept of habitus. Wittgenstein also gave a hint on how to resolve the contradiction between the relatively uniform concept of habitus and the diversity of observable practices and contexts. He implied that forms of life extend to a highly variable number of people. While some contexts are limited to small in-groups, others seem to comprise the entire humankind. Wittgenstein (1989) argued that this is the precondition for understanding people from other societies, cultures and language families. This also implies that there are components of the habitus that are shared by many people and others by very few (cf. Rehbein 2015).

The "chips" or other resources necessary to play the game are referred to by Bourdieu as *capital*. It is immediately evident and presupposed by any theory of inequality that economic capital, especially money, is the key object of inequality. Bourdieu (1984) argues that practices in capitalist societies do not only require economic resources but also knowledge, abilities, certificates, connections, memberships, titles and so on. He subsumed them under the notions of economic, cultural, social and symbolic capital. The disposal of these types of capital, according to Bourdieu, determines the possibilities of action and thereby the social position.

Bourdieu's concept of capital resembles the concept of capital as it is used in economics. However, the concepts of human and social capital still refer to economic entities; they point to the value of resources for the economy. By contrast, Bourdieu's concept of capital refers to the whole of society and to social structure. It interprets resources as prerequisites for status, possibilities of action and access to various social spheres. In other words, the economy is only one field of action among many.

According to Bourdieu, we need to take into account not only the total amount of capital a social group or an individual disposes of, but also the relative strengths of various types of capital and the history of their acquisition (1984: 109). This is usefully illustrated by comparing old wealth with newly acquired wealth. If we compare two owners of big companies with identical wealth, we will find that the one who acquired his wealth more recently usually has far less influence – not only in the economic field but also in most other fields. This is because old wealth is linked to other forms of capital, especially *social capital*. Someone from an old, wealthy family enjoys social connections, which newcomers lack by definition.

Besides lacking such connections, the *parvenu* usually does not know how to behave "correctly". Only people who grew up in a certain segment of society develop a particular habitus. Groups whose habitus is not formed in a distinguished social environment gain entry to a privileged habitus only with difficulty, even if they have the financial means. If we consider the wealthiest segment of society, we might think of rock stars, football players and criminals. They enjoy significant economic capital but lack other types of capital. While it is necessary to have substantial wealth to belong to the dominant segments of society, one also has to know how to behave. In European societies, part of being a member of the social elite is to cherish expensive wines. Newcomers who can afford expensive wine, and value it as a status symbol, nevertheless remain outsiders to the social environment in which the taste for it is developed, even if they have the financial means to acquire it. A football player may not automatically know how to drink fine wine, which glasses to use, how to distinguish a good from a bad vintage, and especially not how to talk about it. Even if he learns all of this, he might still be ignorant of how to blow his nose in such an environment, which politicians to favor and what to know about history and society. Bourdieu subsumed all of these abilities under the concept of *cultural capital*. Apart from dispositions, cultural capital comprises education and professional titles as well as material cultural symbols such as works of art.

In his *Distinction* (1984), Bourdieu focuses on economic and cultural capital. In other works, he distinguishes other types of capital, such as social, symbolic and political capital. *Symbolic capital* for Bourdieu is the prestige conferred by a title, a function, or some other personal endowment as well as the recognition it entails (1984: 291). For example, economic capital does not only enable a person to buy something but also to be revered. An educational title adds to the value of what one says or knowing the president may save you from getting a speeding ticket.

Bourdieu claimed that the distribution of capital and relevant habitus traits lies at the core of inequality in capitalist societies. We agree but we would add the symbolic and the historical dimensions, which we will discuss on the following pages. Apart from this, Bourdieu never really explained how to empirically study habitus and capital. Finally, he assumed that capitalist society is divided into classes which are distinguished by different amounts of capital. We do not agree with this notion of class at all.

Class

In the previous section, we claimed that Bourdieu only studied the surface of a capitalist society. That is because he focused on an old capitalist nation-state, France, and disregarded its history. For this reason, he came up with an unsatisfactory notion of class. The class lines that Bourdieu draws in his *Distinction* (1984) are random and not justified theoretically or even empirically. It is not at all evident that there are classes in capitalist societies – and, if there are, how they can be defined.

The concept of class is usually introduced either descriptively or deductively. The descriptive approach is arbitrary and lumps certain professions or income levels together and calls them a class (e.g. Goldthorpe 2007). Bourdieu (1984) merely drew two dividing lines in his construction of the French "social space". In his work on Algeria, he used income as the principle of division (Bourdieu 1963). The deductive approach applies a theory of society and posits, for example, two antagonistic classes (e.g. Marx and Engels 1964). Neither approach connects theoretical considerations and empirical research properly or manages to explain the reproduction, internal differentiation and transformation of classes in capitalist societies (Rehbein and Souza 2014).

We argue that the notion of class with reference to a capitalist society has to take capital and habitus into account but it is only complete if it includes the historical and the symbolic dimensions. In our research, we started with the assumption that capitalism dismantles classes and other structural hierarchies, a hypothesis, which has been very influential with regard to Germany (Beck 1986). However, we discovered that there are dividing lines in Germany which are seemingly impossible to cross. There is plenty of social mobility within and between the generations but it stops at certain boundaries. These are the limits of a class, which constitute symbolic and moral dividing lines between groups of people in a society. They are part of our definition of class and will be dealt with in the subsequent section of this chapter and in Chapter 4.

Important for our definition of class beyond the symbolic dimension is its cultural foundation. The capitalist transformation is a real revolution but a revolution is not a creation out of nothing. It entails socioeconomic mobility, separates social structure from the division of labor and creates a whole new range of professions for all social groups. But it does not abolish older inequalities; it only transforms them and makes them invisible. Edward P. Thompson (1963) was the first to demonstrate the continuity and transformation of a class with the advent of capitalism in England. Michael Vester enlarged Thompson's approach with regard to Germany. He argued that social milieus in contemporary Germany are successors of precapitalist ranks (Vester et al. 2001: 79).

Thompson and Vester define classes not merely on the basis of capital but interpret them also as *cultures* with a common practice. Their central argument is that practices are not created spontaneously but are passed on through habitualization or training from one generation to the next. On the one hand, these practices and cultures are subject to constant change because they relate to and influence each other; on the other hand, they continue long traditions. This interpretation acknowledges both change and continuity and resolves the contradiction between social structure analysis and everyday history (Vester et al. 2001: 23). According to Vester, Marx and Beck failed to see that the European workers were no fragmented group that organized from scratch but had instead incorporated their precapitalist traditions and adapted them to the conditions of industrial capitalism (133). Instead of classes, Vester therefore speaks of *tradition lines*.

We follow Thompson and Vester in their interpretation of class as culture and tradition line. A class passes on core elements of habitus and capital from one generation to the next and distinguishes itself actively and passively from other classes. Hereby, it erects barriers for mobility and access to specific activities as well as power. On this basis, it is possible to establish classes empirically as the barriers of mobility and of access to activities are the limits of a class. An increase in one type of capital is not equivalent to mobility. Gopal Guru (2012: 47) has demonstrated that an "untouchable" person (Dalit) in India may be able to accumulate all kinds of capital on the free market but still remains excluded from the upper strata. A Dalit millionaire remains a Dalit. Guru (2012: 49) adds exactly in our veins that a casteless person becoming a millionaire has only one structural effect and that is the legitimation of neoliberalism. Most critics of liberalism, including Marx and Bourdieu, were unable to see this because of their focus on capital and labor. The successful struggle for capital renders the mechanisms of social inequality invisible.

Our notion of class is related to Weber's concept of social class (Weber 1972) but is more clearly defined and more closely linked to empirical research. We define class as a tradition line with a common culture which reproduces itself from one generation to the next by passing on relevant capital and symbolically delimiting itself from the other classes. This concept can be operationalized by establishing the limits of social mobility (Rehbein et al. 2015). Where the itineraries of social mobility typically end is the limit of the class.

Individualization, milieus and division of activities

The narcissistic idea of the free individual has been part and parcel of symbolic liberalism ever since Hobbes. Any encounter between an Asian and a Northatlantic society proves that the idea of individualization needs to be defined more precisely as normalization plus formal liberalization. The apparent chaos and lawlessness of traffic in India is as much an example for Asian individualism as John Embree's (1969) famous characterization of Thailand in the 1940s as an individualized society. The free liberal individual is produced in a long process of standardization. A British driver does not have to be forced to turn in the direction he is signaling because he has internalized the system of rules. Most Indians have not.

Michel Foucault (1977) has dealt with the process of normalization in France, which took several centuries. He makes two points that are relevant for our argument. First, the process of normalization also created the individual of symbolic liberalism. Second, the process differed for and in each class. One could say that each class was normalized to fit a specific type. Following Marx, he distinguishes the two classes of bourgeoisie and workers but then also talks about a class of delinquents. This resembles the class structure we have found empirically in Germany except that he, just like Marx and Bourdieu, does not specifically address the dominant class as a separate group.

Foucault shows that the legal system of the new democratic state developed in such a way that it at once normalized all citizens and divided them into different classes. It is based on the principle developed by Hobbes and Rousseau that any legal offense is not directed against specific individuals but against the entire society. It is not the king, a victim or a responsible person who takes charge of the offender but a representative of society. The goal of the legal sanction consists in reintegrating the offender into society as well as normalizing all other individuals by demonstrating the limits of society. According to Foucault, the legal system is only one element in a complex setup of institutions designed to streamline the citizens of the newly democratic state. He calls its functioning "disciplinary power" (Foucault 1977). In contrast to feudal society, power in a democratic society is not designed to oppress or exploit people but to make them useful, to increase their socioeconomic productivity to a maximum. To this end, the highest degree of standardization has to be combined with the highest possible degree of specialization. This is exactly what Adam Smith called for as well.

Like Smith, Foucault argues that there are different classes in the newly democratic society which are supposed to carry out different functions in the division of labor and have different positions in the institutions. It is interesting to note that Foucault referred to the emblematic democratic society, France after the revolution, while Smith was referring to the feudal society of the United Kingdom in the eighteenth century. Foucault demonstrates the persistence of classes and their transformation within a democratic state with regard to the legal system. Although civil law mainly concerned citizens and their property, the system of accusation and punishment mainly concerned the lower classes. Different courts were established to deal with different issues that concerned different classes. Our empirical research shows that this division of classes in the legal system is still largely valid for present-day Germany and Brazil. It is almost a defining feature of the underclasses that their members have been convicted at least once in their life.

We do not think that this system is intentionally designed to oppress the lower classes. No malevolent intention and no conscious action is necessary to reproduce the class structure. The differences are incorporated, contained in the meaning of the socially accepted symbols and transmitted from one generation to the next. Formally, all individuals are equal but their incorporated patterns of actions as well as the social evaluation of these patterns differ according to class. This is hardly visible, not only because of formal (legal and political) equality but also because of the individualization of lifestyles, professions, economic status and personal characteristics.

In principle, all institutions in a formally democratic society are open to everyone. This is due to the democratic idea of equality but also to the economic idea of the increase of productivity or the "wealth of nations". The division of labor is no longer based on the order of classes but on the maximum output. To this end, any labor has to be carried out by the person most suitable for it, by the best. This is exactly what happens. In capitalist societies, the best carry out the most important functions in the division of activities. This seems to be based on merit but it is actually based on class. The members of the highest classes incorporate the patterns of action required and valued for the highest functions in the division of activities. Members of the highest classes occupy the highest functions in the division of activities and define the characteristics required to carry out such a function. They recruit individuals on the basis of these criteria. Unsurprisingly, other members of their class, who embody the same characteristics because they grew up in the same environment, are the individuals who meet the criteria best. They are the best.

This reproduction of class is at the same time riskier and more efficient than a feudal order or a monarchy. As all individuals are formally equal and all institutions are open to everyone, the highest classes have to enter competition. Upward mobility for the lower classes is formally and actually possible. However, the invisibility of the reproduction of class makes it more efficient in the reproduction of inequality than any open inequality. Class position is also more secure because a feudal order is characterized by constant struggles, assaults and even annihilation of ruling families. One could be toppled, exiled or killed at any point in time. In a formally democratic society, any dominant position is based on some kind of achievement, a seemingly objective recruitment of the best. It is legitimized by merit.

The reproduction of inequality becomes even more opaque because of the obvious individualization. There are no visible classes any more, just individuals competing on open markets. These individuals carry out a bewildering variety of activities, which they combine to rather unique life-courses. This has given rise to the hypothesis of a society "beyond status and class" (Beck 1986). Socioeconomic parameters and social position no longer allow for predictions of an individual's lifestyle, let alone concrete choices in everyday life. We agree that predictions of this kind, including those made by Bourdieu (1984), are empirically incorrect. What is worse, they contribute to the invisibility of the mechanisms reproducing inequality. It is precisely the apparent individualization that makes these mechanisms functional. It goes hand in hand with a recruitment for important positions, which is apparently based on merit. Choices are particular and based on rather individual life-courses. However, they hardly affect the reproduction of class. That a manager listens to "proletarian" rock music or that a laborer wears a three-piece suit has virtually no effect on their sociological life-chances.

Still, the apparently individual lifestyles are not random; they bear resemblances on the basis of class and socioculture. Such resemblances constitute social *milieus* (Vester et al. 2001). People of the same class and the same generation have more in common with each other than with other people. This commonality does not consist in merely statistical preferences for this or that but mainly in a similar habitus. The general orientation of individual actions and (supposed, observed or incorporated) traits is the same in many regards for a milieu. We found empirically, for example, that the entire generation of West Germans that was socialized around 1968 has a much more liberal attitude toward society in general and disadvantaged groups in particular than the other generations, or that the entire generation socialized after 1975 in Laos grew into a peasant culture. However, in each generation the class cleavages persist. Even in the German 1968 generation, which acquired certain habitus traits that distinguish it from any other generation, the children of the dominant class acquired a "taste", social knowledge and certain skills that no other class possesses and that are highly valued, especially in the dominant class itself. These traits were prerequisites to access highly valued positions in the 1970s and 1980s. The prerequisites have been transformed since but only the children of the dominant class were capable of attaining them in their childhood.

In this book, we use a rather particular concept of milieu. Vester's milieus are referred to as "habitus groups" or "habitus types" in this book. The habitus is not co-extensive with the socioculture or class. Therefore, we disconnect the term *milieu* from habitus in order to designate hierarchical segments of socio-cultures. More precisely, each milieu corresponds to one hierarchical level in one of the empirically discernable sociocultures. This will be explained in more detail in the course of Chapter 3.

The criteria for recruitment are constantly transformed because the capitalist division of activities is constantly revolutionized. However, the criteria applied by those occupying the highest positions and recruiting juniors to occupy them in the future are precisely those which they teach their children and which their children incorporate better than other persons (Jodhka and Newman 2007). Those persons occupying the highest positions know best what it takes to run the show tomorrow. They want to make sure to recruit people who have what it takes. This is not taught in any family or school, simply because very few people know what it takes to run the show. Of course, the criteria that are applied by the recruiters are still subjective in the sense that they are constructed and incorporated, but they are also objective in the sense that they are unconscious and a product of history.

Members of the dominant class occupy the highest positions and have access to the most valued positions, whereas members of the other classes formally have access to them but are practically excluded because they do not meet the criteria. Which activities are valued and reserved for members of the higher classes is a product of history (Massey 1984: 40). It is somewhat irrational and arbitrary but intelligible and consequential. The marginalized class has no access to markets or even to productive activities, while the lower middle class only has access to the lower segments of the labor market and the upper middle class to the upper segments and to some segments of the capital markets. Only the dominant class has access to all markets without even needing it. The differential value of activities reproduces the order of power and makes it invisible. A CEO or a supreme court judge are mere employees who had to succeed on a competitive labor market like everyone else. But their decisions have an impact on the lives of thousands, which is not the case for the decision of a housewife or a storage worker. And the latter will never apply for a more valued activity, and if they did, they would not be recruited because they do not have what it takes. And from the perspective of the dominant class and the division of labor, this is even true. The members of the dominant class usually do not even need to compete on any market as their activities are often constrained to running a charity foundation or looking after their fortune.

Symbolic reproduction

Our argument is only complete after understanding why laborers or housewives never become CEOs even though they formally can. In capitalism, this is due to a specific form of symbolic domination, which has not been addressed properly by Bourdieu and Foucault. They argued that the entire society shares a dominant discourse, which is the discourse of the dominant class. Furthermore, they also postulated that the unequal distribution of capital is the root of inequality and its reproduction in capitalist societies. We argue that this postulate contributes to the invisibility of the mechanisms at the root of inequality and thereby contributes to its reproduction. The foundation of inequality is not capital but its valuation. More generally, it is the unequal value that is attributed symbolically to activities and habitus traits including the evaluation and devaluation of groups and individuals. The unequal value is contained in the use of symbols, which means in any action.

Empirically, there is no discourse that dominates the entire society. There are very few elements of discourse that are shared by all social groups. In most regards, each milieu has its own discourse and its own sociolect. People classify each other within this discourse, which means that each classification of another person depends on the relation of one's own milieu to that of the other. However, the discourses are not equal as their power to influence the discourses and lives of other groups differs and as the activities and habitus traits valued by the dominant are also valued by the dominated to a certain degree, which is not true the other way around. In other words, the power to define and apply symbols differs according to class. This is also true for other forms of inequality, e.g. between genders or ethnic groups. The symbols used for the dominated and their traits contain a devaluation in themselves, at least in the discourses of the dominant. It is not up to the dominated to change that because they do not have access to the valued positions, traits and discourses.

What is more, the dominated cannot change their symbolic value because they incorporate the negative traits and are not necessarily aware of their social construction. It is considered natural for a woman to be soft and powerless, for the underclasses to perform manual labor, for the dark-skinned to be less intellectual and enterprising or for the societies of the global South to be more corrupt. Any reality check confirms these stereotypes because they have been embodied by the individuals in their respective social environment. Thereby, the traits mentioned are naturalized together with their negative value (Souza 2009). This is why the symbolic universe magically fits social reality even though it is not intentionally constructed by the ruling class for the purpose of domination. Even Bourdieu and Foucault contribute to this symbolic domination by claiming a qualitative difference between more and less advanced societies and by focusing their analyses on the supposedly most advanced nation-state. The empirical fact that France is more productive and less corrupt than Brazil, however, is not proof of modernization theory but of the effectiveness of symbolic domination, which postulates that the value of a nation and its inhabitants should be judged on the basis of productivity and corruption.

Symbolic domination implies that people and their traits have a value. This value is supposed to differ between classes. Instead of socially constructed, it is regarded as being founded on natural reality because the traits are incorporated, as they are an integral component of the person under consideration. There are more and less valuable activities, there are more and less valuable personality traits and capabilities, there are more and less valuable habitus or types of people and there are more and less valuable classes of people. This classification is implied in any hierarchical or unequal social order. It is not specific for capitalism. In capitalism, it acquires two peculiarities. First, it becomes invisible because it is covered up by a surface proclaiming equality and competition. Second, it establishes a hierarchy of values, which is based on supposed moral superiority. We have dealt with the first characteristic in the previous section and the preceding paragraphs. Now, we have to briefly outline the genesis of the capitalist hierarchy of values. Chapter 4 deals with it in more depth.

The hierarchy is closely linked to symbolic liberalism and is largely developed in line with it. Charles Taylor (1989) has analyzed the history of the contemporary concept of the self as a conjuncture of Platonic Christianity, reformation and Enlightenment. Just as we have traced the philosophic root of symbolic liberalism to Hobbes' interpretation of Descartes, Taylor views Descartes as the major inventor of the modern concept of the self, which he calls the "punctual self". Taylor does not deliver another history of ideas but tries to trace how the concept of the self became an integral part of people's practice and emotions.

According to Taylor (1989: 117), Plato installed the rule of reason over the passions, which was integrated into Christianity. The Christian Church called for a taming of the passions and a rationalization of practice. Thereby, Plato's concept of reason did not remain a philosophical idea but became part of everyday practice. It was complemented by Augustine's focus on the inner world and his concept of virtue as something invisible. Descartes followed Plato and Augustine but turned the hierarchy of virtue and reason upside down. While for the Christian tradition as well as for Greek antiquity, virtue (mediating the good) was the highest value, Descartes argued for the precedence of reason (Taylor 1989: 177). Cartesian reason, however, is no longer characterized by specific contents but by a certain method, a rational procedure. This, for Taylor, is the main trait of the "punctual self". The punctual self was the foundation of Hobbes' theory of the state and then strapped of all historical, religious and social constraints by John Locke.

This self is "punctual" because it is not embedded in particular contexts but virtually empty. It can be shaped by disciplined action. Together with Locke's liberal concept of the self, a liberal science, administration and social organization was developed to ensure the disciplining of the self. According to Taylor, this was only possible because the protestant reforms established the rule of reason over the everyday practice and the inner self of the citizens (1989: 159). Inequality was no longer justified and legitimized on the basis of virtue and God.

Therefore, the way was paved for the concept of an egalitarian society consisting of "punctual selves" based on self-discipline, labor and rationalization.

The new, liberal values remain mostly unconscious but are deeply incorporated and institutionalized. They become explicit only in their practical effects. We have not conducted a single interview in Brazil and Germany in which labor did not play a core role for the definition of the self. Neither did we encounter people who are untouched by the "punctual self", which portrays the individual as free, autonomous, independent, self-transparent, conscious and in charge of his or her own choices. This infantile notion of the everyday *Übermensch* is an integral component of our contemporary concept of the self, both for the common sense and for mainstream social science. We believe to be the creators of our values and of our life-courses without taking their social base and their history into account. Our idea of freedom is the easy rider – driving along a well-planned and maintained asphalt road under the attentive eyes of the police.

Taylor subsumed all ideals linked to the liberal concept of society under the term "principle of dignity". It is based on the idea that all equals can potentially recognize each other as such. The principle of dignity according to Taylor is one of the sources of the contemporary self. It goes hand in hand with the punctual self and partly contradicts another root of the contemporary hierarchy of values, namely the "expressive self". The punctual self implies equality and reciprocity, whereas the idea of the expressive self points to the original and singular character of a person. The expressive self is not about identity of social atoms but about the voice of the individual, which cannot be mistaken for anyone else's. Both concepts contradict each other because they both originated in the subjective turn toward the inner being in Christianity but point to contradictory ideas of the moral good. Discipline and identity on the one hand are contrasted with originality and difference on the other (Taylor 1989: 375). The idea of the expressive self reinterprets affects as feelings by infusing them with meaning and spirit. The inner self is no longer a field threatened by irrational and unholy impulses but a sphere of the depth of meaning. Linked to this reinterpretation is the transformation of moral judgment into something where reason and feeling have to join forces in order to distinguish right and wrong.

While the principle of dignity distinguishes the worthy members of society or the decent working classes from the marginalized underclasses or Foucault's delinquents, the expressive self is reserved for the upper classes who are not only hard workers but also possess an individuality that deserves expression. These principles guide our evaluation of classes as groups of people who are naturally equipped to be what they are. Taylor's hierarchy of values does not explain all classifications and inequalities but it points to the most important dividing lines in all capitalist societies, be it Brazil or Germany. More importantly, his approach enables a critique of the principles of humiliation and inequality, which appear natural to us and remain invisible.

We found an additional dividing line at the top of society that neither Bourdieu nor Foucault found in their studies. Taylor does not come up with a notion of the self that could characterize the dominant class either. That is because none of them ever had access to this group. It is the class of people who we never see. It consists of the wealthiest capitalists, often members of old dynasties rarely appearing in the Fortune 500 or Forbes lists. It also comprises old nobility or royalty, sometimes large landowners and some members of the political elite, especially in authoritarian regimes. This class does not have to labor and does not have to prove itself – as worthy or expressive. It does not enter into the same type of competition as the rest of society and does not have to achieve anything because it has basically achieved everything from birth. We characterize this class as *aloof*. The following chapters describe it in more detail.

Conclusion

Almost all contemporary nation-states have undergone the capitalist transformation. They have a similar surface, as they are supposed to consist of disciplined individuals who compete for functions, objects and money with differing results that can be measured in terms of capital. This surface is associated with symbolic liberalism, which is imported to some degree by all capitalist nation-states. Under these conditions, the structure of social inequality, its roots and its mechanisms become invisible. Inequality becomes a matter of capital and can be moderated or even neutralized by its redistribution.

We have argued that, in contrast to symbolic liberalism, the capitalist transformation perpetuates precapitalist hierarchies. It partly transforms earlier hierarchies into social classes, while these earlier hierarchies partly continue to persist underneath and next to the classes as sociocultures. The capitalist transformation entails a particular class structure, which divides people into "useless", generally "useful", particularly "useful" and outstanding classes. As these classes are transformations of earlier hierarchies, they are entangled with local peculiarities and form configurations, which are specific for each nation-state. The analysis of social inequality consists in the disentanglement of sociocultures, precapitalist hierarchies, their transformation and social classes. This is what the following chapters try to do with regard to four very different nation-states from four world regions, namely Brazil, Germany, India and Laos.

Each of the chapters tries to give an overview of contemporary structures of inequality in the respective nation-states. At the same time, each chapter focuses on a different aspect of the general approach to inequality outlined above. The study of Germany focuses on class, habitus and capital. The chapter on Laos traces the capitalist transformation and the emergence of classes, forms of capital and relevant habitus traits. The bulk of the part on Brazil is devoted to the study of symbolic inequality. The chapter about India relates class, sociocultures and the symbolic dimension to caste and identity. In the final chapter, we try to compare the four different cases and link them to a more general theory of capitalism and inequality.

2 Classes and habitus in Germany

Germany is a country which is considered to be Western and part of the core. It is one of the nation-states with the best values for the mainstream indicators of development, economy, democracy and in some dimensions even inequality. Therefore, it is a suitable case study for inequality in a country with a long capitalist history and a stabilized social structure. We will see, however, that Germany also experiences very stable structural inequality. This chapter tries to show that social inequality in contemporary Germany is based on invisible social classes, which are reproduced through classification. The classes are heirs of precapitalist ranks and constitute durable cultures. Their prehistory is no longer clearly visible in Germany. For this reason, we will study the prehistory and emergence of capitalist classes with reference to the case of Laos in the next chapter.

It is surprising how stable the structures of inequality have remained in Germany despite the massive revolutions of the twentieth century. There is a significant inheritance of social position from one generation to the next. We characterize the structural conditions of this inheritance as *reproduction*. Reproduction means stability of the social position over time, especially as far as generations are concerned. Even if people have entirely different jobs, interests, friends, abilities and lifestyles than their parents, they "inherit" their parents' position relative to the rest of society. This has been Bourdieu's (1984) main argument with regard to social structure. We confirm this argument and add that relative positions based on the unequal integration of precapitalist ranks have changed very little during the past centuries because the issue of inequality has been reduced to a merely economic problem.

The following study of Germany focuses on the reproduction and composition of classes.[1] It is based on a collaborative empirical work carried out between 2009 and 2015. This work comprised almost three hundred qualitative life-course interviews of 30 to 120 minutes duration and a quantitative survey of 2,950 cases representative of the German population in terms of gender, age, educational title, place of dwelling and migration background. In the final stage of this research, 61 representative qualitative interviews were conducted; these form the basis for the interpretations in this chapter.

The chapter first demonstrates that social inequality in a capitalist society has to be understood as the reproduction of a class position. Class position in turn is not defined by a single indicator, such as profession or wealth, but by a combination of factors which have to be determined empirically. On this basis, classes and their dividing lines become visible. The dividing lines between classes in Germany are discussed in the following section and are explained in more detail with regard to Brazil in Chapter 4. The chapter then summarizes the distribution of capital between the different classes. The subsequent sections are devoted to habitus types and ethos groups in German society. The chapter closes with a brief review of the intersection of class and female gender.

Classes

In terms of education and profession, most Germans resemble their parents even though there has been an "educational expansion" and a "skills revolution" in the last quarter of the twentieth century, which means that many young Germans would have a higher educational title than their parents. Against this background, the reproduction of educational titles is even more surprising than persisting educational inequality. Inequality is illustrated by the fact that only 6 percent of Germans whose fathers are unskilled laborers have a high school diploma, as opposed to more than 80 percent of those whose fathers have a university degree. This means that merely a tiny percentage of those coming from disadvantaged families have the slightest chance of completing university and entering the higher strata of the labor market.

The reproduction of educational title is illustrated in Table 2.1. It shows that about half of the people in our quantitative sample have the same educational degree as their father. If we consider that women would tend to follow their mother more than their father, and that husband and wife do not always have the same educational degree, the correlation approaches 70 percent. As mentioned, this has to be interpreted against the background of increased educational opportunities and exigencies. Today, a nurse would possibly need a BA in nursing, whereas his or her parents might have been manual laborers or did not need a university degree if they were nurses as well.

The reproduction of educational inequality is enhanced by informal factors. Education in the family comprises a lot of skills and "personal traits" that are

Table 2.1 Correlation of own with father's highest educational degree

	Father: basic	Father: middle level	Father: high school	Father: tertiary
Basic	57%	16%	11%	7%
Middle level	30%	56%	31%	23%
High school	4%	12%	41%	17%
Tertiary	9%	16%	17%	53%
Total	100%	100%	100%	100%

vital for access to high school, clubs and evaluation. These characteristics are distributed differentially according to class. There is a strong correlation between parents' educational degree and informal factors, which can be designated by the term "cultural capital". For example, only 15 percent of the respondents with a basic school degree (Hauptschule) or less say that their parents had a library at home, whereas not a single respondent reports going to museums or the opera during childhood.

We can observe the same reproduction with regard to profession. More than 50 percent of all Germans share the same occupational class with their fathers (following Oesch 2006). In addition, 70 percent choose a partner from the same occupational class. Once again, these numbers have to be seen against the background of tertiarization, which means that most children of manual laborers born in the last quarter of the twentieth century did not become manual laborers because these jobs have disappeared.

The degree of these correlations may be surprising but the plain fact of reproduction certainly will not astound many readers. It is intuitively evident that people acquire a lot of skills but also resources from their parents. Like father, like son, goes the proverb. However, this insight is limited to *isolated* items. The core of our argument concerning the reproduction of classes is directed against the isolation of factors. We argue that each factor reinforces the others but remains a merely statistical item in itself if we do not study the *mechanism* of reproduction and the *relation* of all factors to each other.

For this reason, it would be theoretically wrong and empirically unsatisfactory to define or measure class on the basis of one factor, such as economic capital or educational degree. Even though the correlations between class membership and these two factors are very strong, they remain statistical. Not every member of the German (or any other) upper class has a PhD or is excessively rich (all through his or her life). But he or she will certainly display most characteristics of his or her peers at any given point in time. Therefore, we have to look at the combination of characteristics.

First, we realize that only certain combinations of factors occur in reality while others are rare or even nonexistent. For example, it is rare that the daughter of an unskilled laborer gets a PhD. But it is virtually impossible that she also embodies high culture, acquires a substantial portfolio of stock shares and marries a prince. Second, we have to understand the entirety of the possible combinations in order to explain the reproduction. Third, we have to include the entire life-course together with those of the ancestors. A CEO may become unemployed, and a football player rich – but usually only for a limited period of time. What is almost fully excluded is the reproduction of this abnormal state in the next generation.

In order to understand class as a varying combination of evolving factors, we use a methodological approach, which is more stochastic than statistical. There are children of CEOs without high school diplomas, and children of unskilled laborers with a PhD. But there are almost no children that share few characteristics with their parents and their childhood peers. Any characteristic may be absent but the majority will be present. No fixed combination of characteristics defines reproduction and class. Therefore, we need a concept that grasps this varying combination of changing characteristics. We found this concept in Wittgenstein's *family resemblance* (Wittgenstein 1984: aphorism 65ff.). Wittgenstein illustrates the varying combination of changing characteristics with regard to a family: all members of a family have some things in common, such as the nose or the intonation of certain words, but no two members share exactly the same traits. It is possible to explain many similarities but it is not possible to reduce them to general categories or characteristics. The same is true for the socially relevant characteristics of a human being. In order to find the existing combinations and the social "families", we use an appropriate methodological tool, namely multiple correspondence analysis. This tool allows us to identify and weigh the joint existence of social characteristics.[2]

We determined the relevant characteristics through the interpretation of our three hundred qualitative life-course interviews: What was important for social mobility or stability? What was experienced as a lack? What was similar between people with a similar position or origin? We generally follow Bourdieu (1984) in regarding capital and habitus as the most fundamental characteristics regarding social inequality. Apart from economic and cultural capital, however, we also consider social and symbolic capital as vital. Our samples revealed income and wealth as appropriate indicators of economic capital and the educational title as a good indicator of cultural capital. In these dimensions, we do not differ from most other research on inequality. We use the social position of friends, the parents' social environment and membership in clubs as indicators of social capital and capture symbolic capital through honorary titles and the family name. All of these indicators are linked to the basic variables of the life-course. We define them as social origin (profession and educational titles of parents and grandparents), parenting styles and schools attended. Finally, we add those aspects of the habitus that our interviews revealed as significant and unequally distributed: social activities, subjective importance of achievement, self-confidence, discipline, flexibility, a sense of order, subjective importance of leisure and willingness to learn. The combination of all of these factors varies from individual to individual but presents a certain configuration of family resemblances for each class. The corresponding characteristics are passed on within the class from one generation to the next.

Our criteria match the most important institutional steps in a German's life-course. It begins with the social origin of the family and is then modified and augmented by parenting style, important values in the family, the type of school, the peer group, hobbies and organizational membership. At birth, one enters the parents' class like a magnetic field. The later influences usually, but not always, correspond to this class and reinforce its incorporation.

Once we established the classes, we found that it is virtually impossible to cross the dividing lines between them in contemporary Germany. Mobility happens, if at all, only for a limited period of time or within one generation; a mobile individual usually remains an abnormal case within his or her family. We discovered three such dividing lines within German society: the line of dignity, the line of expressivity and the line of aloofness. As we found similar lines in Brazilian society, we discuss them in more detail with regard to Brazil in Chapter 4. The dividing lines contribute to the existence of social classes that are reproduced over many generations. In our three hundred qualitative interviews, we did not find a single case of mobility across class lines – even though mobility within the class is common. Each class has its own culture, habitus and life-worlds. Since classes should be understood as traditions lines, they are not only defined by capital but also by habitus and symbolic systems.

The three dividing lines constitute four social classes that we call marginalized, fighters, established and aloof. The marginalized remain excluded from many sections of society, especially a constant and decently remunerated profession. They dispose of a small total volume of capital and mostly have a fatalistic or hedonistic habitus. The fighters are the core of society and form the bulk of the laboring population. The established carry out the leading functions and dispose of a large total amount of capital. The aloof are aloof in the sense that they are virtually separated from the rest of society and especially from labor. They are the large owners of economic capital and usually have old family trees (Piketty 2014).

The dividing lines are not identical with the differences between institutional segments or the division of work, between occupational classes or the division of labor or between habitus groups, but their reproduction is mediated by these. This mediation contributes to the opacity of the class lines, as recruitment and the development of the habitus do not take place in a closed, ranked society any more but in formally open and equal processes.

As our samples were representative in many ways but not constructed on the basis of our class model, we can only estimate the size of the classes in Germany. A reasonable estimate for the marginalized class is less than 20 percent, for the fighters more than 65, for the established less than 15 and for the aloof a maximum of 0.1 percent. The class of fighters consists of two tradition lines, one rooted in the old working class and one in the petty bourgeoisie (cf. Vester et al. 2001). We can distinguish between aspiring and defensive fighters. They do not form separate classes as there is mobility between them. This is even more so for the two tradition lines within the established class, namely the intellectual and the economic faction. This distinction becomes increasingly blurred. It is significant and interesting that Theodor Geiger (1932) found similar classes in the 1920s and already observed that the highly skilled laborers were passing the old middle class of the employees and shopkeepers. We can trace our five contemporary tradition lines via Vester's analysis back to the 1920s.

Figure 2.1 shows the result of a multiple correspondence analysis (MCA) comprising all indicators we consider relevant for the identification of class membership. While some indicators are spatially close or even lumped together, others are at the opposite ends. This distribution hints at the family resemblances of combinations. It is likely that all characteristics that are spatially lumped together will exist simultaneously in an individual. All those characteristics that

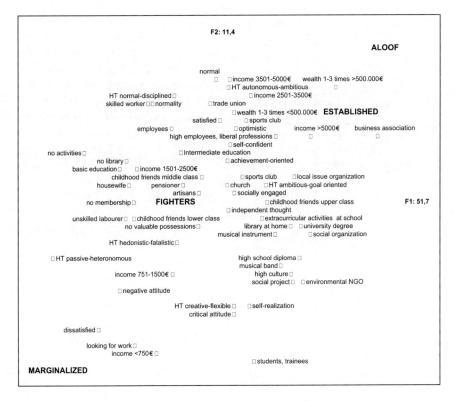

Figure 2.1 Multiple correspondence analysis (MCA) of classes in Germany

are close together are likely to appear in a class. The social classes are distributed across the space in the illustration diagonally from the bottom left to the top right. The aloof are on the top right and the marginalized on the bottom left.

While the term "class" is no longer fashionable in academic discourse and at the same time current in everyday language, it is often used as if it refers to a real entity or even an agent. We wish to stress that class is a construction even if its characteristics and the dividing lines are real. Class does not exist in the same way as a person or a thing. And it is not the principle of explanation. The explanation of inequality rather consists in the explanation of the classes, which in turn consists in the relation of classification, habitus, capital and selection against a historical background.

Classification

Any explanation of social inequality has to show how social classes and the dividing lines between them are produced in and through social practice. The decisive mechanism in this production is classification. We would like to think that classification in democratic societies is rooted in the equality of chances and objective criteria. All of us would say that for any function we would select the objectively most appropriate person. But who is objectively most appropriate? Of course, it is the person who has the best abilities for the function. We designate this criterion as *meritocratic*. And we argue that the meritocratic discourse renders the structures and mechanisms of inequality invisible. Inequality appears to be the result of individual choices.

The meritocratic discourse is well established in Germany. It is rooted in the European liberal traditions and claims that human beings exist as independent and free individuals who make choices between all socially available options. According to this view, anyone is free to contribute to society, achieve something and reap the fruits of this achievement. In one of the interviews we conducted in Germany, a young member of the established class says: "The things that really matter in life everyone can achieve, no matter in which class he lives or from which milieu he originates, where he lives, of course there is an equality of opportunities."

The meritocratic view interprets the attainment of important values, such as a good job and a lot of money, as result of a purely individual achievement in a competition under the conditions of equality. The social structures, parents, education, social environment and family networks supposedly do not matter. Everything results from one's own individual actions. A university professor says: "Persistence is necessary, one has to work for a long time. What I have achieved, is of my own making."

The meritocratic view implies taking responsibility for one's life and making one's choices individually. "I remember a phrase my father used to say, which I hated: Help yourself, then God will help you. And now I have to admit that this has been one of the most important phrases in my life." This established interviewee interprets his father's attitude as noninterference and his current situation therefore a result of his own achievement. It does not seem to matter that his father paid for his education and valuable hobbies, possessed a lot of books and taught the son important communicative skills. All of these seemingly irrelevant details came up in the interview.

In this way, the structure of society is turned upside down. People actually are different. Many of these differences are socially produced and correspond to a person's class. The differences are socially classified and influence access to activities and goods, which are also socially classified. People develop skills and resources in a class structure and receive access to highly valued activities and goods according to their skills and resources. With a high likelihood, the son of a CEO possesses exactly those skills and resources that are necessary to access highly valued goods and activities. Even his emotional setup is most suitable to carry out a leading function in society.

In Germany, achievement is defined on the basis of labor to a larger degree than in India or Laos. People classify each other by their "contribution to society", which rests upon their labor. This has consequences for the meaning of life. Who one is – for others and oneself – is largely defined by one's profession (or its absence). In our interviews, the question about a family member was usually first answered by their profession. We were surprised to find that this mindset characterizes the entire population of Germany except the aloof class.

Our main point is that the focus on formal wage-labor not only influences the meaning of life but also implies a classification of people. A secretary states this very clearly: "There are no high or low classes. I respect anyone who does a good job." Only a laboring person is a valuable human being. The value can be measured by one's contribution to the "wealth of nations" (Smith 1998). And it also qualifies for a certain share of it. A "good job" deserves respect and remuneration, a bad job less so, and no job means no contribution and deserves no respect and no remuneration. The classifications good job, regular/bad job and no job are core aspects of the dividing lines between the classes. The half of the population that does not yet, or no longer, perform wage-labor is classified according to their presumed contribution, while unemployed family members (usually women) are subsumed under their partners – but they "deserve" less respect.

Labor is the central component of the concept of achievement in capitalist societies. It also means normality in Foucault's (1977) sense. A laboring person is a normal, decent, respected, disciplined member of society. The absence of labor rarely makes a person sinful or lazy but creates a subjective longing for a distant, romanticized dream. A homeless person says: "Sundays are the worst because one does not know where to go. Everything is closed. . . . But on weekdays I am here . . . basically sitting here talking. What can we do?" The unemployed suffer from their "uselessness". Very few of them "take advantage" of the welfare state. They rather want to be normal and labor like everyone else. The lack of a job also strips them of their social dignity.

The existence of almost half of the German population is defined by the presence of wage-labor. This is interpreted not as a dream or self-realization but as necessity. "Then I have to go to work. Eight hours. And every day from nine to five [laughs]. It pisses me off every day." The same employee also says whether he prefers leisure or labor: "Well, I used to think leisure. Now, I unfortunately know that they cannot be separated. That is, one has to earn one's leisure." He accepts the "social contract" and acknowledges that one has to contribute a share to the wealth of the nation. The contribution justifies leisure and reaping the harvest. It also legitimizes one's own existence as a "normal" life and confers social dignity.

At the same time, the majority of the laboring population does not cherish professional life. One would give up the job and do something else right away if the chance came up. A cook says, "my hard work is not being acknowledged", an assessment shared by many. If the meaning of life is partly or even mainly defined by one's labor and if one contributes one's share to society, one expects to be acknowledged. According to Max Weber (2011), the acknowledgment in the early days of Western capitalism consisted in the fruits of labor, which presumably indicated the love of God. The bulk of the population, however, reaps few fruits and cannot consider itself chosen. Labor is rewarded with leisure and dignity but does not entitle one to power and grace.

God's grace is limited to a minority of the population who mainly belong to the established class. The founder of a small IT company says: "I am a workaholic. There is always the danger that I work too much." This danger does not extend to the majority of the population who would only work too much in order not to become unemployed. The labor of the privileged few is acknowledged in terms of respect and remuneration. Their life is not about the existence of a job as a necessity but their job is part of a larger life project as a work of art – or expressivity. Even they are normalized; however, they also have to contribute their share. Usually, they experience a lot of pressure on the job. The keyword is "career". A retired CEO claims: "It was impossible to reduce the career in any way, it was just necessary."

Only the very top of society remains untouched by the process of normalization and the necessity to perform wage-labor, both for financial and for social reasons. None of our unemployed interviewees classified themselves as lazy; only a rich and aristocratic heiress was confident in stating that she had been "lazy all my life". She does not have to earn her existence or contribute her share. Some top managers, movie stars and financial wizards have acquired more wealth than the heiress – but they have to perform labor and have to define themselves on this basis. This is not the case for the top stratum of the social hierarchy, which is aloof.

Capital

Each social class disposes of a specific and characteristic combination of capital. Class cannot be defined by one form of capital alone. But even the combination of types of capital does not suffice to define a class. First, the value and even the structure of each type of capital changes constantly. Manners may be less important today as a component of cultural capital, but cultural capital in general is probably more valuable today than it was fifty years ago. Second, capital has to be used effectively, which requires an appropriate habitus. Third, for any type of selection, habitus may be more relevant than capital.

This section studies the distribution of capital among the classes in contemporary Germany. We found the differences in economic and cultural capital that were used by Bourdieu (1984) in his analysis of French social structure in the 1960s to be relevant in Germany today: wealth, income, educational title and incorporated knowledge of high culture. Apart from that, social capital, which has been neglected in Bourdieu's study, seems to be very important. We operationalize social capital as peer group, parents' social environment and organizational membership. Finally, the symbolic dimension has never been understood adequately by Bourdieu, first in the shape of classificatory construction of class division lines discussed in the previous section and also in the form of symbolic capital.

It is no surprise that wealth differs between the classes. An almost surreal gap separates the aloof from the rest of the population. In order to understand the distinctions between the other classes, we have to take the type of wealth into account (see Table 2.2). A lot of Germans own real estate, which they use for

Table 2.2 Operationalizing capital

Economic	Cultural	Social	Symbolic
Wealth: real estate	Educational degree	Membership	Name
Wealth: shares	High culture in childhood	Friends in childhood	Honors
Wealth: other tangibles	Hobbies in childhood		
Income	Parenting style		

Table 2.3 Wealth and class: property worth more than € 500,000

	Real estate	Tangibles	Shares
Marginalized	0%	0%	1%
Defensive fighters	1%	0%	0%
Aspiring fighters	3%	1%	2%
Established	10%	0%	3%
Aloof	100%	100%	100%

Table 2.4 Social class and professional class

	Prof. class 1	Prof. class 2	Prof. class 3	Prof. class 4	Total
Marginalized	44%	56%	0%	0%	100%
Def. fighters	8%	32%	53%	7%	100%
Asp. fighters	0%	5%	60%	35%	100%
Established	0%	0%	0%	100%	100%
Aloof	0%	0%	0%	100%	100%

themselves. Only the aloof and the very rich established use real estate as an investment. If we look at investment in shares or objects, the dividing lines become even more obvious. 45 percent of the established own real estate worth less than 500,000 euros and 10 percent own real estate worth more than that. Almost 90 percent of the marginalized, 73 percent of the defensive fighters and 64 percent of the ambitious fighters own no real estate. Sixty percent of the established, 49 percent of the ambitious fighters, 22 percent of the defensive fighters and 7 percent of the marginalized own shares. In contrast, all of the aloof own wealth worth more than 500,000 euros, in all categories (see Table 2.3).

The differences in income are a bit less pronounced than those in wealth but also rather striking. We have observed that almost all marginalized have to live off a monthly household income of less than 1,500 euros, while most established and all of the aloof dispose of a monthly household income of more than 5,000 euros. Even more interesting than the income distribution is the relation between social class and occupational class, as depicted in Table 2.4.[3] There is a striking

Table 2.5 Class and highest educational degree

	None	Basic	Middle level	High school	Tertiary	Total
Marginalized	1%	71%	26%	2%	0%	100%
Def. Fighters	0.2%	50.8%	45%	2%	2%	100%
Asp. Fighters	0%	7%	37%	19%	37%	100%
Established	0%	0%	11%	26%	62%	100%
Aloof	0%	0%	0%	0%	100%	100%

Table 2.6 Class and social capital: which class did the parents of your childhood friends belong to?

	Upper class	Middle class	Lower class	Total
Marginalized	2%	77%	21%	100%
Def. fighters	2%	86%	12%	100%
Asp. fighters	3%	92%	5%	100%
Established	9%	86%	5%	100%
Aloof	100%	0%	0%	100%

correlation, which links social class not only to income but also to the level of incorporated cultural capital.

We already pointed to the fact that the higher classes have a higher educational degree, which in itself almost becomes an indicator of social class (see Table 2.5). In addition, the higher educational degree strongly correlates with competences and preferences in the field of high culture. All of those in the aloof class and most of the established have learned to play a musical instrument at home. If we focus on the correlation between educational degree and musical instrument, the picture becomes even clearer. None of those without an educational degree have learned to play an instrument, whereas almost all of those with a PhD have acquired this skill in their childhood.

Our survey also shows that the foundation of social capital is already laid in childhood, which means by the parents. For example, during their childhood most of the established have been members of organizations where they did not only acquire cultural capital but also friends from the same social background, i.e., social capital (see Table 2.6). In contrast, 92 percent of the marginalized have not been members of such organizations. Apart from the formal setting for the formation of social capital in organizations, the informal networks of childhood friends are highly unequal as well. This is clearly expressed in the table. In the qualitative interviews, most members of the established class indicated that they made use of these childhood and youth networks for their professional career, directly or indirectly.

Table 2.7 Class and social capital: are you a member of an organization?

	Yes	*No*	*Total*
Marginalized	32%	68%	100%
Ambitious fighters	44%	56%	100%
Defensive fighters	58%	42%	100%
Established	66%	34%	100%
Aloof	100%	0%	100%

One could argue that these clear correlations are invalid because they are circular, as we used each of the correlating factors as indicator of our social classes. This argument is only partly valid, as we do not define the classes on the basis of single indicators but as complex combinations of indicators. Theoretically, each *single* correlation could be very weak. The strength of all correlations proves the significance and comprehensiveness of class. It also demonstrates that our class model is rather adequate.

Habitus

Bourdieu did little to operationalize the concept of habitus. A core part of our research consisted of finding ways to study it empirically. We initially used the approaches of the "documentary method" (Bohnsack 2014) and "habitus hermeneutic" (Lange-Vester and Teiwes-Kügler 2013), both of which are elaborate attempts to operationalize Bourdieu's habitus concept with the aim of constructing (ideal) types of habitus on the basis of qualitative interviews. We adapted these methods in the course of our research until we were able to encode the interviews on the basis of "elementary categories" – indicators which have highly varying values for different types.

We used a representative sample of sixty-one qualitative interviews to identify twenty-seven elementary categories, the combination of which delivers habitus types by clustering in a multiple correspondence analysis in the same way as in our construction of classes. Our final encoding matrix was comprised of four dimensions. Nineteen elementary categories were conceived of as binary oppositions and eight as tendencies, which are the first two dimensions. The oppositions point to synchronic traits and the tendencies to diachronic orientations. Eight of the nineteen binaries function "vertically", i.e., point to class differences, and eleven "horizontally", signifying differences within classes or between generations. In the third dimension, we correlated the eight tendencies with the available information on grandparents, parents and parenting style in order to determine the options for social mobility. Finally, we looked at contradictions and contingencies as very few habitus are entirely coherent and ideal-typical (Lahire 1998).

Table 2.8 List of relevant habitus traits

Goal and achievement oriented	Autonomous and ambitious	Normal and disciplined	Creative and flexible	Passive and heteronomous	Hedonistic and fatalistic
Self-confident	Self-confident	Order and cleanliness	No order and cleanliness	Not socially engaged	Leisure
Investing money	Goal-orientation	Normality	No normality	Not self-confident	No order and cleanliness
Optimistic	Sovereign	Not open to change	No discipline	Not open to change	No discipline
High culture in childhood	Optimistic	No self-realization	Self-realization	No activities in childhood	Freedom
Socially engaged	Autonomous	Discipline		Pessimistic	

The elementary categories were then used for the interpretation of our quantitative survey. Combined with theoretical considerations and statistical analysis, the interpretation resulted in twenty-six traits or dispositions, which can be considered relevant for the construction of habitus types in German society. We subjected these traits to a multiple correspondence analysis, which is displayed in Figure 2.3. The clustering of traits points to likely combinations in real habitus. Table 2.8 lists those habitus traits that are most relevant for the construction of each (ideal) type.

The quantitative and qualitative analyses do not use exactly the same traits and do not deliver exactly the same types. This is due to the fact that qualitative and quantitative data are different. Even though the following paragraphs will draw only on the quantitative analysis, we claim that the qualitative analysis is not only chronologically primary but logically more fundamental. First, the qualitative interviews are open and richer in information. Second, the survey questionnaire cannot be constructed without previous knowledge of elementary categories, which in turn have to be either deductively presupposed, as in much of Bourdieu's research, or inductively elaborated out of qualitative material, as in our approach.

The multiple correspondence analysis of the quantitatively operationalized habitus types constitutes a space whose extremes signify the defining characteristics of socially effective differences (see figure 2.2). In the German case, the space is structured horizontally between "autonomy and sovereignty" on the one hand and "heteronomy and lacking sovereignty" on the other (see figure 2.3). The vertical extremes are "normality" at the top and "self-realization" at the bottom. Diagonally, "activity and achievement" are in the lower left corner, while "passivity and lacking interest in achievement" characterize the opposite end of the spectrum. This diagonal opposition corresponds to the

Normality
Discipline
Passive
Autonomous
Heteronomous
Active
Self-realization
Creativity

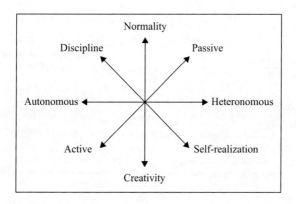

Figure 2.2 Vectors of habitus traits in Germany

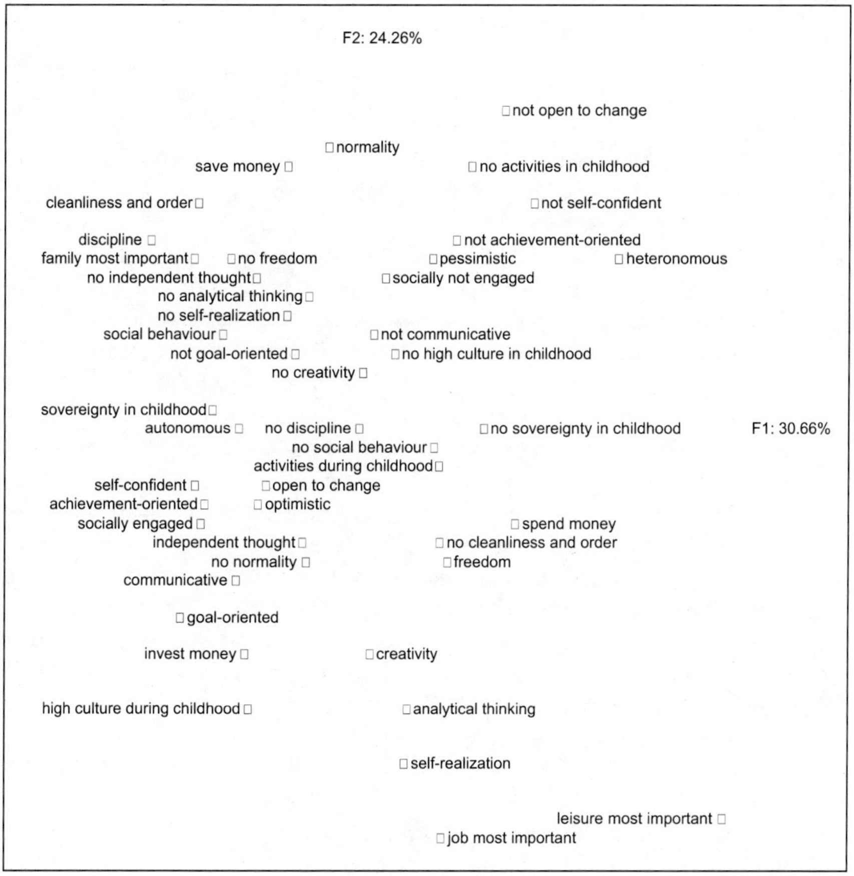

F2: 24.26%
not open to change
normality
save money
no activities in childhood
cleanliness and order
not self-confident
discipline
not achievement-oriented
family most important
no freedom
pessimistic
heteronomous
no independent thought
socially not engaged
no analytical thinking
no self-realization
social behaviour
not communicative
not goal-oriented
no high culture in childhood
no creativity
sovereignty in childhood
autonomous
no discipline
no sovereignty in childhood
F1: 30.66%
no social behaviour
activities during childhood
self-confident
open to change
achievement-oriented
optimistic
socially engaged
spend money
independent thought
no cleanliness and order
no normality
freedom
communicative
goal-oriented
invest money
creativity
high culture during childhood
analytical thinking
self-realization
leisure most important
job most important

Figure 2.3 Multiple correspondence analysis (MCA) of habitus types in Germany

Table 2.9 Habitus types

Habitus type	Percentage in sample
Goal and achievement oriented	14.4
Autonomous and ambitious	19.0
Normal and disciplined	26.4
Creative and flexible	20.0
Hedonistic and fatalistic	14.5
Passive and heteronomous	5.8

division lines between the classes: the habitus of the aloof is located in the bot-tom left, whereas that of the marginalized would be on the top right.

We have found six habitus (ideal) types, which can overlap and crisscross in the sense of Wittgenstein's family resemblances (see Table 2.9). The fuzziness and flexibility of the habitus is not an exception but rather the rule in social practice, especially if the context does not correspond to primary socialization. However, it is extremely unlikely that two contrary habitus types are incorporated in the same body.

The goal and achievement oriented habitus type, comprising about 14 percent of the population, partly overlaps with the autonomous and ambitious type and is farthest from the passive and heteronomous type. Its core is characterized by self-confidence, optimism and a tendency to engage in organizations. It is the classical upper-class habitus that experiences a lot of high culture in early educa-tion. Other important characteristics that appear a bit less frequently are the determination to succeed, goal-orientation, an independent mind and strong communicative abilities. A defining characteristic of this habitus type is the readiness to invest financially, which is linked to the favorable financial situation, in which this type usually grows up and lives.

The autonomous and ambitious habitus type is, like the first type, most strongly opposed to the passive and heteronomous type as well as to the hedo-nistic and fatalistic type. It comprises almost 20 percent of the sample popula-tion. This type is also self-confident and optimistic but furthermore, it is characterized by goal-orientation, sovereignty and a strong longing for autonomy. Determination to succeed and openness for change as well as strong commu-nicative skills and an independent mind are secondary characteristics. This type distinguishes itself from the first type in its orientation to family and social values. However, it is an upper-class habitus as well.

About one quarter of our sample population can be subsumed under the normal and disciplined type. It is most strongly opposed to the creative and flexible type as well as to the hedonistic and fatalistic type. The normal and disciplined type embodies "German" values, such as cleanliness and order, normality and discipline. The core is defined partly by the rejection of self-realization and change. Secondary characteristics are an orientation toward the family and social matters as well as an inclination to save money. An independent mind, freedom and creativity are not cherished. Very few people with this habitus have experience with high culture during their childhood. Preserving the social position of the family is more important than upward mobility. It is a habitus of the middle classes.

The creative and flexible type comprises about 20 percent of the population. It overlaps with the hedonistic and fatalistic type. Both are the paradigmatic individualists. However, the creative and flexible type defines itself through its profession and is more upper class than the hedonistic and fatalistic type. It is most strongly opposed to the normal and disciplined type, rejecting values like cleanliness and order, normality and discipline. Social matters play only a minor role, while creativity, an independent mind, freedom and the job are most important. The main orientations are creativity or analytical thinking.

Close to 15 percent of our sample fits the hedonistic and fatalistic type. It is located at the opposite end of the goal and achievement oriented type but distinguishes itself most pronouncedly from the normal and disciplined type. Freedom and leisure are the defining traits of this type, as well as the rejection of cleanliness, order and discipline. Secondary characteristics are self-realization and the inclination to spend money. It shares an individualistic tendency with the creative and flexible type but does not define itself through a profession. For the hedonistic and fatalistic type, a job is only a means to finance one's leisure time.

At 6 percent, the passive and heteronomous type is the smallest of the six habitus types we identified. Its core is defined negatively: the absence of social engagement, of self-confidence, of openness to change and of optimism. There was not only no experience of high culture during childhood but usually little organized activity of any kind. Even the secondary characteristics are mostly negative: lacking achievement-orientation, autonomy, sovereignty and communicative skills. A positive definition is the inclination to spend money. This is a habitus of the lower classes together with variations of the normal and disciplined type and with the hedonistic and fatalistic type.

The habitus types are clearly anchored in the class structure but have to be distinguished from it. The passive and heteronomous as well as the hedonistic and fatalistic appear almost exclusively in the classes of the marginalized and the defensive fighters and not at all in the established and aloof classes. At the other end of the spectrum, the aloof and 40 percent of the established can be subsumed under the goal and achievement oriented habitus type. The three other habitus types mainly appear among the fighters.

That each habitus type appears in more than one class seems to contradict our claim that there are insurmountable dividing lines between the classes. There would, however, only be a contradiction if we did not distinguish between habitus and class. The primary habitus is formed in early childhood, usually and mostly in the immediate surroundings of parents. Then the person enters a series of institutions that are vertically segmented. The hierarchical segments, however, do not correspond neatly to the division of ranks as in European feudal society. For example, general school (Hauptschule) is attended by the marginalized and fighters, while fighters, established and aloof may attend high school (Gymnasium). During their joint time in the same institutional segment, the children develop similar habitus traits. This continues into professional life. For example, the profession of a lawyer does not comprise members of a single class. Idealistic criminal lawyers often earn less than a skilled laborer, whereas the directors of law firms that organize company mergers belong to the top of the occupational hierarchy.

In spite of the heterogeneous structure of schools and professions, people develop similarities in their habitus if they perform the same activities over an extended period of time. Thereby, similarities and differences between habitus types emerge that do not correspond to the hierarchy of classes. Only a minority of people remain exclusively in institutional segments corresponding to their class for their entire life. For this reason, only a few people develop a habitus whose traits only appear in the same class. Even the primary habitus is not purely a class habitus (cf. Lahire 1998).

Bourdieu (1984) and Vester et al. (2001) draw the class dividing lines between habitus groups. According to them, several horizontally delimited habitus groups form a class. Our analysis contradicts this typology. One of the reasons for this contradiction consists in the fact that the upper and the lowest classes are grossly underrepresented in Bourdieu's and Vester's studies. Our analysis would be rather different as well if we had only surveyed three classes. Another reason for the contradiction is theoretical and concerns the relation between class and habitus. From our perspective, class is reproduced through various institutional segments, which in turn produce most of the habitus traits. The habitus types would only correspond to the social classes if class structure and division of work were identical as they were in European medieval societies. It is an important characteristic of Western capitalism that this is not the case.

We can differentiate between the elements contained within the habitus in more detail by distinguishing habitus from cultural capital. In the first chapter, we already pointed to the fact that both concepts overlap but are not identical, as not all dispositions of the habitus can be used as capital. It is important to note that those dispositions that can be used as capital correlate most strongly with class membership. Furthermore, the primary habitus is deeply rooted in the childhood milieu and thereby corresponds significantly to the parents' class. The secondary habitus is differentiated through institutional segments and subcultures and individual strategies of distinction. Therefore, it corresponds much less to class.

According to our quantitative survey, basic orientations that were acquired in early childhood correlate strongly with class, such as goal-orientation, communicative skills, self-confidence and optimism. Goal-orientation rises in a linear fashion from 19 percent in the marginalized class to 100 percent in the aloof, communicative skills rise almost linearly from 18 to 50 percent, and optimism rather linearly from 16 to 100 percent. The distribution of cultural capital is similarly clear and unequal. While merely 8 percent of the marginalized were exposed to high culture in their childhood, this is true for 100 percent of the aloof. An education style defined by humiliation and violence, on the other hand, is almost exclusively limited to the lower classes.

Ethos

People are not mere images of their class position. And they do not passively incorporate the conditions of their surroundings. They also adopt an active and reflexive attitude toward their habitus, class position and the social conditions at large. The basic attitude toward society and one's own life is delimited by one's class position but cannot be *deduced* from it. It develops in reaction to the perceived characteristics of the nation, group, surroundings, self, etc. This reaction is rooted in the habitus but does not remain preconscious in the same way as other dispositions. It results from active reflection as much as from tradition. Following a few scattered remarks by Bourdieu (1984), we wish to call this general attitude *ethos*.

One's ethos results from an adaptation to factual conditions. As the conditions are similar within the class, ethos is also rooted in class membership and therefore identical for many members of a class. However, just like the habitus, an ethos goes beyond class lines and at the same time does not cover an entire class. It is closely linked to the habitus but not identical with it either, as reflection may differ from action and perception.

We can distinguish three layers in the fundamental attitude toward society. One is shared by most members of society. For Germany, Foucault's concept of disciplining characterizes this layer very well. More precisely, the values of labor, adaptation and achievement are spread widely and form points of reference. They influence the meaning of almost everyone's life and the evaluation of others except for those of the aloof. The value of each class is mostly determined by its "contribution" to society, which rests upon its labor and is measured by its fruits. However, the classes have different life chances and cultures. Therefore, the effects of the disciplining process differ according to class. In the same way, the possibilities of enhancing one's value are limited along lines of class division. A hairdresser may rise to become an owner of a chain of salons – but he or she will not become a top CEO or member of the high nobility.

The second layer results from the first. It consists of the active and passive evaluation of classes, especially the three dividing lines of dignity, expressivity and aloofness. The third layer is the reaction to the first two; this is the one we call ethos. Ethos exerts a significant influence on everyday practice, but in contrast to habitus it is more a consequence, rather than a presupposition, of practice. Whoever is born into the marginalized class develops a habitus of high culture, a circle of influential friends or the ability to invest substantial economic capital only under very unlikely circumstances, for example through adoption or very devoted parents. The class can react to its hopeless position in several

Table 2.10 Class and ethos

Class					
Aloof	Satisfied	Enthusiastic			
Established	Satisfied	Enthusiastic	Adapted		Critical
Fighters			Adapted		Critical
Marginalized			Adapted	Resigned	Rebellious

ways. It may resign, rebel or fight. These are the three prevailing ethoi in the marginalized class.

In total, we found six main ethoi in contemporary German society (see Table 2.10). Four of them cross class boundaries significantly, while resignation and rebellion are mostly confined to the marginalized class. The most numerous ethos is the active participation in one's own disciplining process, which we call ethos of adaptation. About half of the German population incorporates the values of labor and achievement and accepts its social position. The majority of fighters, a third of the marginalized and a few established share this ethos. A larger part of the established class and almost all of the aloof react to their position with an ethos of satisfaction. A few fighters, many of the established and some of the aloof develop a very engaged attitude toward society and their life. They have an ethos of enthusiasm. The marginalized either have an ethos of adaptation or a negative attitude of rebellion or resignation. The negative attitude also appears in the classes of the fighters and the established but then becomes, due to the options of these classes, more active. We call this attitude an ethos of critical distance.

It might seem as if the marginalized should deny the prevailing social structure and the value of labor and its fruits, while the fighters accept it and the established welcome it. These tendencies actually exist but they do not characterize the classes. A critical attitude toward society and its values is most widespread among the fighters and established, whereas a large percentage of the marginalized strive for integration into the existing social structure. Not all established welcome the social reality and not all excluded are negative. We will see that these attitudes differ significantly in Laos and Brazil.

Most people do not have a single ethos at any given point in time and certainly not throughout the duration of their lives. They do not have the same attitude in all situations and surroundings. It is only due to the homogeneity and stability of social environments that a somewhat coherent ethos develops. If the circumstances change, the ethos is likely to change as well – a bit like changing clothes with the weather. We adapt our clothes to the weather but we do not change our clothing style entirely each time. And we usually share this style with many other people in our social and spatial vicinity. In the same way, we share and change our ethos with other people who live under the same conditions as us.

Gender and partnership

Gender inequality may be more pervasive than inequality between the classes but class is more fundamental in capitalist societies, as each class has its own structures of gender inequality, but each gender, on the other hand, does not have its own class structure. In each class, it means something else to be a man or a woman – or another gender. There are, however, gendered practices and values that extend to the entire society. For this reason, men have certain social characteristics in common across class boundaries, and so do women. Erving Goffman (1979) coined the term "gender classes" to grasp this phenomenon. In this section, we will look at the other end of the spectrum, class genders, especially in the female habitus of each class.

Most women share a common space at school, at work, in the household and in public spaces, and are subjected to similar expectations. But the similarities are differentiated according to class, because the classes mostly choose different schools, jobs and organizations. Each class is further differentiated into habitus groups and ethoi. The habitus types outlined earlier do not only differ in their dispositions but also in their use as capital. Therefore, each habitus type uses gender rather differently, and vice versa.

According to the social commonalities of most women, there are some "normal" female characteristics that are shared by all classes. These include the relevance of sexual attractiveness, niceness, an inferior position to that of the man and family orientation. These traits are incorporated mainly by girls (who later become women, of course). Very few boys and men in our interviews talked about household tasks or their family and especially fatherhood without prompting, while almost all women devoted some time to the topic of motherhood. Despite many decades of emancipation, the primary social function of women is reproduction and child care. The woman is oriented toward the family, the man toward the outside world.

Apart from the commonalities, women incorporate something like a class gender. This means that the class culture influences the way a habitus is gendered and used as capital. For a marginalized woman, her body is the most important capital, which defines her social value to a large degree. Violence and abuse in childhood are much more common here than in the other classes. Social relations and the future are uncertain. Under these conditions, there are not only few financial resources but also few emotional ones. A reliable husband can be the source of both. It comes as no surprise that fidelity is a much more important criterion to define an ideal partner than in the other classes.

Conditions in the class of fighters are more stable than those of the marginalized but in both classes, motherhood is a core value for women. This includes a traditional division of sexual labor. One fighter says: "Of course, I do the household. I am his wife." In contrast to that of the marginalized, this position is reliable. Unlike the marginalized class, the girls also grow up under stable conditions. As women, they are able to plan ahead because they have always had a future that can be planned. The basic temporal structure consists in the division of labor, leisure and family. For these women, the family is more important than the other two.

For established women, the body is less relevant in terms of a resource for sexuality and labor. They grow up in an emotionally and financially stable and usually supportive environment. Their future can be planned and they actively structure their time. Life is interpreted as a comprehensive work of art, in which motherhood, labor, sexuality, family and partnership are *optional* components. Most established women are in a position to support themselves financially.

Aloof women may be less emancipated than established women as they have to contribute to the reproduction of social position and the family. They do not do this as individuals but as members of a larger network. Their life is structured and well planned but not a work of art.

Most people choose their partner from the same class. This is not surprising since the overwhelming majority of individuals with whom one interacts come from the same class. A bit more surprising is the observation that one tends to classify persons from one's own class more positively than others. Both observations apply even more accurately to habitus groups. Finally, partnerships within the habitus group make sense because one tends to get along better with someone who shares the same values, language, patterns of actions and thoughts. These are people who grow up under similar conditions or at least in the same class. They also have to incorporate the values of this class.

The most appropriate partner for a marginalized woman is someone who can provide the physical, emotional and financial support that is necessary for most women in this class. It is interesting to find that marginalized women are most open in their criteria of the ideal partner and most likely to marry across habitus and class boundaries. For the female fighters, a male partner has to value the family and have a job. An established partner is expected to be attractive much more than in the other classes. He also has to have an active physique and an appropriate amount of all types of capital. In the aloof class, family origin and respect are the most relevant factors. Fidelity and mutual support are relatively more important for marginalized men in choosing a partner, while the relevance of attractiveness is most pronounced among men of the upper classes.

The relation between class and gender is similar in Brazil, if not more pronounced and clearly delimited. However, we will see that in Laos, genders are differentiated much less according to class than according to socioculture and ethnicity. This is due to the strong persistence of precapitalist sociocultures in Laos in comparison to Brazil and Germany. We have not yet studied the intersection of gender with other inequalities in India but the configuration will certainly be different there.

Migration

Most studies of inequality have treated migrants as a residual category or ignored them. Hearing the word migrant, we would tend to agree with this approach because we immediately think of a poor person or a refugee. However, migrants can be found in all classes. They do not form a parallel world but an integral component of German society even if they are not fully integrated subjectively and often objectively. In terms of capital and habitus, it is almost impossible to distinguish between Germans and migrants.

Literature usually differentiates between migrants who moved to another country, and persons with a migration background whose parents fully or partly come from a different country. Some migrants are classified as foreigners if they do not get German citizenship. We will use the terms foreigners, Germans with a migration background and Germans in the following paragraphs even if these terms are problematic. The first two groups together make up about 20 percent of the German population and almost the same percentage in our research samples.

In general, migrants will enter the German class that is similar to their class of origin. When comparing Germans with foreigners and people with a migration background, four points seemingly deserve a mention. They concern the habitus, capital and country of origin. First, any person entering German society has to have a disciplined habitus including the ability to plan, to control oneself, to value achievement and to labor. If this is lacking, the person will not be integrated or will remain in the marginalized class. Therefore, a marginalized person coming to Germany will usually remain marginalized. And somebody from a Western country is more likely to have the "appropriate" habitus than someone from the global South.

Second, foreigners and people with migration background have to bring or to acquire the same amount and structure of capital as Germans. This capital not only determines class membership but is also relevant for integration into German society at large. In order to identify with German society on a subjective level, symbolic capital is most relevant.

Third, the amount of capital brought from another country largely influences one's chances in Germany but it has to be translated into German capital, both literally and figuratively (Nohl et al. 2014). Grosfoguel (2004) has argued that the classification of a migrant depends on the ranking of his or her country of origin in the global power hierarchy. If the migrant comes from a country less powerful than Germany, his or her capital will be devalued. This is also true for the official recognition of cultural or even symbolic capital. The maximum value of a foreign title of education is equality with the German title but usually it is recognized by the authorities as only partly equivalent (Sommer 2015). This is especially true for titles from "remote" countries as their titles and standards are different. And any difference results in an official devaluation. Business tries to raise the value of foreign titles in its specific field in order to attract qualified labor. As this results in a decrease of the exclusivity of German titles, the administration counters this tendency.

Fourth, the subjective feeling of integration differs with class, but not in a linear fashion. Germans with and without a migration background feel more integrated into society if they belong to a higher class. The higher the class, the more integrated people feel. For foreigners, however, almost the opposite is the case. While all of the established and aloof Germans and 86 percent of established Germans from a migration background feel well or very well integrated into German society, this is the case for only 50 percent of the established foreigners.

All migrants lack some capital in comparison to their German peers. For the higher classes, it is possible to make up for some of this by investing other types of capital and more effort. However, differences on the level of habitus always remain. It seems that these are most seriously felt by members of the established class. At the same time, all marginalized, whether Germans or foreigners, face the same difficulties in participating in society. Their subjective feeling of integration is the same. Eighty percent say that they feel well integrated into German society.

The marginalized migrants do not differ from the Germans in their struggle for recognition and participation. Discipline, long-term planning and structured processes are problematic. The fighters with migration background do not differ much from their German peers either except in terms of the recognition of their educational titles. They are oriented toward labor as well but are integrated into the labor market with more difficulties. The differences between foreign and German established are subtle in their life-courses but rather manifest in terms of integration and acceptance.

Reproduction of the social position

From the perspective of the individual, the social structures sketched in the previous section function a bit like magnetic fields that attract or repel the individual. With birth, one enters such a field, which usually is the parents' social environment. The longer one remains in the field, the more one incorporates its patterns. This is how one learns to become a member of society and to live in it. At the base, the environment comprises all of humankind and then, to a certain degree, the entire nation-state but mainly the immediate class culture.

With increasing age, it becomes more and more difficult to incorporate the patterns of other social environments in the same way. It becomes more difficult to adapt to the culture of another country, to learn a new language, to change one's habitus and to fit into another class. One is increasingly urged to move in environments for which one's habitus was formed. This has a cultural reason as one cannot learn all the predispositions that the members of one's age group from another class have incorporated from early childhood. And it has a social reason as it becomes more and more challenging to gain access to other social environments.

Every member of German society seems to have equal chances to access any institution. In fact, this is true only for specific segments of these institutions. Access to each segment is restricted by classification and selection. A cleaning woman does not only not become a CEO because she simply chose another job, but because she never got the elements of capital and habitus that give her access to a good elementary school and good grades. Thus, she misses the opportunity to be selected for high school (Gymnasium). By this time, at the latest, the higher segments of the labor market remain closed for her.

The requirements of the labor market and the structure of each group's or even each person's capital change constantly. But at any given point, the members of the highest class control access to the highest segments of any institution. In this position, they can make sure that their children acquire the most relevant capital and habitus and that they can recruit their peers for the highest positions. Even if the recruitment process is entirely transparent, formalized and functional, the recruiters will most likely classify the applicants according to criteria that they themselves have embodied (Jodhka and Newman 2007).

In the course of life, one increasingly adapts to the objective possibilities that one's class opens up. Bourdieu (1984) has called this process "amor fati" (social ageing). That means adapting one's wishes and hopes to the perceived facts and developing the opinion that one never wanted anything else than what one actually has and is. This process is not individual but it is shared by a group and in many regards by the entire class.

According to our research, the acquisition of important abilities, such as mastery of the German language or self-confidence, depends strongly on the conditions within the parental household. This household is never a singular case but a variant of the class. Even the spatial environment is not an island but part of a community, which is similar to others in many regards. As a child, one may still dream of completely different and unreal conditions but with age, most people start to accept that their options are limited. As they often do not even know the real-life conditions of other classes, they neither dream nor conceive of a completely different life. Many of our interviewees have stated that they do not know members of higher classes, while the established often point to the fact that they do not know members of the lower classes.

Bourdieu interpreted the process of social ageing in a rather mechanical fashion as the passive adaptation to objective conditions. We have to take into account that these conditions constantly change and that the adaptation is a result of active strategies. Most people have a choice at any given moment between several institutions and functions. This choice is linked to the general attitude toward society, which we have analyzed as "ethos". The attitudes are a reaction to the perceived social life-chances. Social ageing is differentiated not only by class and habitus but also by ethos.

Conclusion

That German society has such a pronounced and persistent class structure comes as no surprise to theoretically oriented sociology. Most classics of the discipline seem to agree that societies that have not experienced any massive upheaval for a longer period of time tend toward a petrified class structure (Marx 1953; Schumpeter 1955; Keller 1963: 38; Weber 1972). Our study on Germany adds nothing new to this insight. However, we take a position in the theoretical debate on the systemic roots of classes. We argue that the class order is more fundamental than capitalism and economic change (Rehbein and Souza 2014).

Functional elites in Germany are largely recruited from the established class. They are separated by an almost insurmountable wall from the aloof class. The wall became permeable in the twentieth century only in the wake of the end of Nazi rule. The contemporary aloof class consists mostly of families that trace their position back to the nineteenth century or even the Thirty Years War. Empirically, the successful elites, the new rich and the upstart capitalists have had almost no access to this class during the past decades (Hartmann 2007). The reproduction of class domination prevails over all concerns of the division of labor.

This does not mean that an analysis of capitalism and the division of labor becomes superfluous, as we argue in Chapter 6. On the contrary, all classes have to reproduce their social position via the division of labor today. Germany is not a feudal society any more. Each individual has to use his or her capital and habitus to reproduce the social position. Through the institutions of the division of labor, upward social mobility is possible for anyone, at least in principle. But the chances of mobility vary with capital and habitus – and are therefore minimal. The holders of the best functions in society define the criteria for accessing these functions, usually come from the highest class, and almost exclusively recruit their peers to be their peers.

Thus, the entire class structure is reproduced even though it contains risks for the aloof class as on each level and in each institution, mobility for members of the other classes is possible. This mechanism of reproduction is in many regards safer than in feudal society, where inequality was openly visible, as the mechanism remains opaque. Society focuses on economic criteria and capitalism. Getting rich means to have "made it". The everyday as well as the scientific criteria of classification confirm this view. But economic improvement precisely changes nothing in the class order.

The interaction between habitus and classification results in the creation and reproduction of persistent tradition lines. The revolutions in the division of labor and constant mobility render the reproduction invisible and anonymous but more efficient than in feudal society, where open struggles and physical threats made reproduction more difficult. The meritocratic myth, which is shared by most social groups, comprises the idea of a fair competition of free and equal individuals whose success can be measured in economic capital.

Notes

1 Apart from the authors of this book, the German research team consisted of Benjamin Baumann, Lucia Costa, Simin Fadaee, Michael Kleinod, Thomas Kühn, Fabrício Maciel, Karina Maldonado, Janina Myrczik, Christian Schneickert, Eva Schwark, Andrea Silva, Emanuelle Silva, Ilka Sommer and Ricardo Visser. This chapter draws on the research conducted by this team, part of which is published as Rehbein et al. (2015).

2 This tool resembles Latent Class Analysis (LCA) used by Savage (2015). It differs insofar as LCA suggests certain classes, while MCA just shows a clustering but does not suggest how to interpret it. However, the theoretical background of both approaches is similar.

3 The classification of occupational classes follows Daniel Oesch (2006). Oesch distinguishes low-skilled and unskilled occupations (in our table, class 1), vocationally and generally trained occupation (class 2), semi-professional occupations (class 3) and professional and managerial occupations (class 4).

3 The capitalist transformation in Laos

The preceding chapter demonstrated that there are four classes in Germany, which are divided by invisible boundaries of social mobility. The classes comprise five historical tradition lines, which are no longer apparent. It seems as if social inequality in a country like Germany can be studied without reference to pre-capitalist structures. This chapter will show that capitalist classes are heirs of precapitalist hierarchies.[1] It argues that the capitalist transformation in Laos gives rise to social classes. At the same time, colonial, socialist and even precolonial social structures persist as sociocultures.

The argument is based on two decades of empirical research in Laos and more than five hundred qualitative interviews. The final sample for this chapter consists of eighty life-course interviews with representatives of all sections of Laotian society conducted between 2012 and 2015.[2] Ethnic minorities and remote areas are quantitatively underrepresented, but not excluded. A questionnaire survey carried out in 2015 partly makes up for this. This survey comprises 648 cases and almost all questionnaires were completed in face-to-face interviews. Quantitatively, peasants are underrepresented in the survey, which means that remote areas are also not sufficiently included but the variation suffices to warrant generalizations. The survey includes 175 peasants or about 25 percent of the sample, whereas peasants compose about half of the Laotian population.[3] The rural sample also takes account of ethnic variations but does not cover a representative number. Furthermore, all interviews were conducted in Lao, which is a second or even foreign language for some of the respondents. The rural survey comprises peasants and farmers as well as officials, teachers, traders and farmers. The urban survey is approximately representative of professional groups, age groups above 14 and the two sexes.

The chapter will first outline the layers of social structure that persist in contemporary Lao society as well as the impact of the colonial transformation, the independence movement and the capitalist transformation. The second section focuses on the relation between capitalist classes and precapitalist structures. It also traces the way in which citizens of Laos are entering the capitalist culture and social structure. The final part studies habitus groups in Laos, which differ from habitus groups in a country like Germany, as they are rooted in different historical periods or social structures.

Sociocultures in Laos

Practices change slowly, institutions even more so, and social structures at large are rather persistent. However, these constant tiny changes amount to significant differences over the course of generations. In rapidly changing societies, children and parents fail to understand each other because they are rooted in different sociocultures. Earlier generations have incorporated practices, norms and values of a different historical time and sometimes a different social structure all together. This is true of contemporary Laos. Reproduction, rapid change and persistence of earlier patterns of behavior combine to create a peculiar layered configuration.

Laos has experienced three major historical transformations in its recent past: the imposition of colonial rule from 1893, followed by a protracted struggle for independence, a socialist revolution in 1975 and the gradual introduction of a market economy beginning in 1986. Like China and Vietnam, Laos retains the political system of a one-party state under the leadership of the socialist politburo, while transforming the economy and many associated institutions into a capitalist system. The respective conditions under royal/colonial rule before 1975, under quasi-Stalinist rule after 1975 and in a rather liberalized environment since the mid-1990s differ very strongly from each other but were partly experienced by one generation.

Laos has been composed of a complex mosaic of ethnolinguistic groups, forms of life, environmental conditions and power relations for many centuries. A group that is dominant in one area or nation-state will be dominated in the next, a group dwelling in the mountains here will dwell in the valleys there, and wet rice here will be replaced by slash and burn there. This mosaic has evolved historically through migration and adaptation (Higham 1989). The complexity has persisted even within the framework of the nation-state up to this day. In any given district, one is likely to find several languages being used and some people who do not even speak Lao, the Tai-Kadai language constructed as the national language under the French. Tai-Kadai speakers have made up more than half the population of Laos since French intervention, with Mon-Khmer speakers comprising another third, Miao-Yao 10 percent and Tibeto-Burmese, Viet-Muong and recent immigrants making up the rest (Sisouphanthong and Taillard 2000).

A conflict between Bangkok and Vientiane ended in the defeat of the Lao-speaking King Anu and his deportation to Bangkok in 1828. Vientiane was depopulated and the principalities of Luang Prabang, Vientiane and Champassak came under Siamese domination, while much of the mountainous terrain to the northeast of these principalities was annexed by Annam and Tongking. At the time, the French already held a trading post in Cochinchina, regarded as a relay port for trade with China. From this outpost, the French hoped to gain access to China via the Mekong river, which runs from China past Vientiane to Cochinchina.

The European turn to imperialism and territorial rule in the nineteenth century led to the French annexation of all of Vietnam and Cambodia. From there, the French moved their sphere of influence west into Siam. In 1893, the local ruler of Luang Prabang asked French officers exploring the Mekong for help against Chinese marauders, who were pillaging the principality still under Siamese domination. The French seized the opportunity and transformed Luang Prabang into a protectorate. Step-by-step, other principalities were integrated into the protectorate. The annexation was legitimized by the claim that the principalities were "Lao" and had been unjustly seized by Siam. The French integrated the Lao principalities and provinces between the Mekong and the Annamite mountain range into their "Indochinese Union" and transformed them into a state called "Laos".

At that time, the French had already recognized that this area was not of much use for their colonial empire. The Mekong was not suitable as a gateway to China. Even the depletion of natural resources was not viable, as the topography of Laos made any significant endeavor very costly. The country was landlocked, mountainous and extremely underpopulated. In 1910, Laos had only around 800,000 inhabitants (Stuart-Fox 1997: 42). By far the largest percentage of the population were peasants living in small villages. Apart from the court and its administration, only a small fraction of the population dwelled in towns.

At the time of French intervention, the peasants may have had different languages and traditions, but shared similar living conditions and social structures. The rural village around 1900 had a fairly clear social structure, which was mainly determined by kinship (Bourlet 1906). There seems to have been a clear hierarchy according to age, sex and specific abilities (Condominas 1962: 2). The elders, the males and the monks – if there were any – as well as the village head commanded more respect than the others. However, this was not a strict class hierarchy but closely connected to personal relations, as most of the villagers were relatives (Potter 1976: 52). Their respective social position and power was hardly disputed. As the relative social position was tied to the respective person, one could speak of a *personal social structure* based on kinship. Much of this is implied by the Lao term for "village", which is *baan*. The term aims more at the social organization than at the physical setting. It is a structured community of people with close cultural and social ties that is not bound to a specific place and constantly changes its composition as people enter and leave the family. For many villages, this remains true up to the present day, even if they were not ethnically Tai *baan*.

In principle, every villager can perform any practice. However, there are specialists in many villages for particular tasks: village head, brewer, musicians, shaman, healer/midwife, blacksmith, possibly traders and in many Tai villages a monk or two. These are not professions, as the specialists are peasants in the first place, but the tasks are linked to particular people with special abilities. This function usually entails additional respect for the person – even if the register of age and gender prevails (Condominas 1962: 99).

The Lao village today is usually located along a waterway or a road, the village of an ethnolinguistic minority usually on a hill or hillside. Most villages depend on rice. The rice fields are near the village and in most ethnolinguistic groups are cultivated in household units. In the valleys, wet rice is grown, whereas slash-and-burn cultivation dominates in the hills. Therefore, the ethnolinguistic minorities overwhelmingly practice shifting cultivation but many Lao peasants have at least some stretches of slash-and-burn fields as well. Most households have a few animals, especially chickens, grow fruit and vegetables and collect additional materials and food in the forest. The compound of the household and a wet rice field, in most villages, belong customarily to the individual couple or family but good agricultural land is always subject to struggles and debates.

Village culture could be described as *subsistence ethics*. This term was coined by James Scott (1976) referring to peasants in densely populated areas. Even though Laos has been very sparsely populated, many of the characteristics Scott used to define subsistence ethics apply to most peasant villages in Laos. Peasants' interest focused on having enough until the next harvest, not on having as much as possible. They achieved this via mutual aid (reciprocity), by reinforcing family ties and traditionalism. They aimed at survival and security, not affluence and profit. Reciprocity, family orientation and traditionalism subsumed under the term subsistence ethics characterize village society in Laos.

Subsistence ethics and personal social structure characterize the peasant population up to the present. There are some differences between the ethnolinguistic groups, most of which can be attributed more to the circumstances than to an ethnic character or culture. Tai-Kadai and many Mon-Khmer villages have weak organizational structures beyond the nuclear family, while Miao-Yao and other Mon-Khmer are organized into extended families, clans and sometimes lineages.

Supralocal trade between villages dates as far back as the Stone Age (Bayard 1984). However, it did not significantly alter subsistence ethics, as the economy was still based on local, noncommercial agriculture. Some of the trade relations may have been on equal terms but there has always been an unequal relation between sedentary and nomadic groups (Higham 1989: 59). There also emerged an inequality between valley and mountain peoples (cf. Leach 1970). Many of the permanent villages in the valleys lay at important nodes of communication and/or places with valuable resources, such as salt, metal or fish (Bayard 1984). The valleys also allowed for a more productive generation of food, especially wet rice.

Some of the villages hosted small markets and some of the market villages developed into towns (Higham 1989: 99, 210). People in the towns began to specialize in either agriculture, trade or a craft. Later, the specialization was linked to social structure, which became hierarchical and was even expressed in the layout of towns: each profession resided in a particular quarter, with the court, the main monastery and the market occupying the center.

The towns subjected some of the surrounding villages and extracted tribute from them, sometimes in exchange for protection. Permanent but unstable relations of dependence, subordination and domination developed out of these

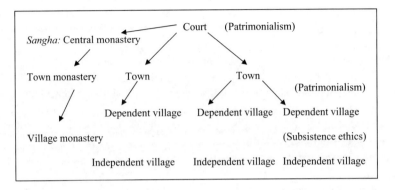

Figure 3.1 Baan-muang structure

configurations. In the Tai context, an urban center with several dependent villages is called *muang*. A number of towns could also become dependent from a larger urban center. *Muang* relations implied loyalties of minor entities to major entities, i.e., of villages to towns and of towns to a court – and sometimes of courts to a king or even an emperor. The principalities could be described by the indigenous terms *baan-muang* (Raendchen and Raendchen 1998). In the *baan-muang* structure, the lesser entities – the *baan* – guarded some independence, especially if they were geographically remote from the centers – the *muang*. The smaller *muang* in turn depended on a larger *muang* and a princely court could dominate the entire structure (see Figure 3.1).

The main character of the relation was exchange of tribute and manpower against security. Loyalties shifted frequently according to the ability of the center to guarantee security and stability. The Buddhist order was to some degree integrated into the structure, while to some degree it formed a parallel structure. Which ethnic group was dominant and which was dominated depended on the local configuration. Inequality existed between valley/sedentary and mountain/nomadic, not between ethnic groups. Furthermore, internal village structure and culture were not deeply affected by the integration into a *muang* (Doré 1980: 191). This only changed with French intervention; previously not all villages were integrated into a *muang*. Many were too difficult to reach. Others constantly shifted allegiance or paid tribute to various overlords at the same time.

In a *muang*, most people were not actual relatives. They were just immersed in relations of loyalty and subordination similar to family relations in the social structure of the village. However, everyone in a family grows up and thereby rises in status, while this is much less possible in the *muang*. The *baan-muang* is a social structure that creates a hierarchy of social groups. In principle, the social position is hereditary and does not change in the course of one's life. A peasant remains a peasant and an aristocrat is born with the privileges of the nobility.

As the town usually was the marketplace and hosted the court, social differentiation mainly took place in the towns. There were factions inside the court and in the population, as well as an increasing division of labor. Superiors tried to accumulate as many bonds of loyalty as possible to enhance their position while inferiors tended to look for superiors who could guarantee security. Just as subsistence ethics characterized the culture of the village, *patrimonialism* was the prevalent culture of the *muang*. Norman Jacobs (1971) used Max Weber's term patrimonialism to characterize the relationship between inferior and superior in Thailand, which was similar to that in Laos at the time. We might continue the use of the term patrimonialism even though it is culturally unspecific and therefore too general (and thus, flawed). More appropriate for our context could be the Tai term *phu-yai* culture. *Phu yai* is a superior, *phu noi* an inferior. It expresses the relation of dependency and subordination that characterizes the patrimonial *muang*.

The most important supralocal institution of precolonial times certainly was the Buddhist order, the *sangha*. The *sangha* was part of the *muang* structure but it also formed a parallel structure in and of itself. In the towns, Buddhism was used by the rulers to consolidate their position (Terwiel 1975: 13). The Laotian *sangha* was organized either exactly parallel to the secular administration or even as a component of it (Zago 1972: 42).

The urban population under the French combined the earlier *muang*, Chinese and Vietnamese traders, Vietnamese administrators and the French dominant class. At any given time, only a few hundred French administrators stayed in Laos, almost exclusively in the largest towns. The French mainly relied on the Vietnamese for jobs within the administration. The Lao were confined to the lowest ranks and the ethnolinguistic minorities were entirely excluded from the administrative body. This policy intentionally created an ethnic hierarchy. Trade and services were dominated by the Vietnamese and Chinese, who in most towns soon outnumbered the Laotian population. Before the arrival of the French, social mobility seems to have been limited. All leading positions were monopolized by the aristocracy, whose members were interrelated (Halpern 1964: 18). The French first drew on this aristocracy for their administration but then imported Vietnamese and finally began to introduce schools to educate Lao administrators (Gay 1995: 234).

In 1954, the French lost the decisive battle against Vietnamese independence fighters under communist leadership at Dien Bien Phu. At the following Geneva Conference, Vietnam was divided into a communist North and a quasi-colonial South. Laos became an independent constitutional monarchy and the communist fighters were given the two northeastern provinces bordering on North Vietnam as a quasi-independent state. In these times of the early Cold War, the US supported the governments of South Vietnam and Laos against the threat of communism. One could argue that this support drove all three nation-states of Indochina into the communist bloc.

US involvement in Indochina basically increased under each president until it reached its climax in the late 1960s with 24/7 bombing of the zones of communist influence. American domination basically replicated French colonial society. Of course, the military, foreign and domestic, acquired a much larger relevance. And the economy catering for the needs of an occupant army became much more integrated into the American-dominated world economy than the colonial economy had been. Finally, the physical destruction caused by the war seems beyond imagination. Almost every family lost at least one member during the war and many families were displaced. But the most important impact of American intervention on social structure was the underground preparation of a socialist society. It happened in the areas occupied by the communist inde-pendence fighters and was then more or less extended to the areas previously under the Royal Lao Government in 1975.

The withdrawal of Western forces from Laos in 1973 left a vacuum of power, which was slowly filled by the communist party. The communist party proceeded step-by-step until the People's Republic was proclaimed on 2 December 1975. In December 1975, the country was physically destroyed, without any economic foundation and completely disorganized. A large part of the population – numbering no more than three million at the time – was displaced, the war had destroyed much of the little infrastructure the French and Americans had built, and almost no industry existed apart from the beer and water factory, tobacco plants and some workshops. A wide strip of Eastern Laos was deforested, poisoned with agent orange and covered with mines and unexploded ordnance. And the state coffers were empty. The money flow from the US had stopped, while inflation stood at 50 percent. Most businesses closed down, and many leading administrators and affluent groups fled abroad with their money and knowledge. It is estimated that of 120,000 government employees in 1975, only three thousand were left in 1976 (Doré 1980: 152).

Under these conditions, the other communist countries were the only viable option for assistance, especially since North Vietnam had received help from the Soviet Union. Laos mainly reverted to a peasant economy (Evans 1990). Possibly a higher percentage of the population than in the nineteenth century lived in the personal social structure according to subsistence ethics (cf. Phom-vihane 1985: 106). As the majority of the socialist cadres had been peasants before joining the party, they were rooted in subsistence ethics as well. Even many teachers, administrators, officers and police were recruited from the rural population after the revolution. The groups rooted in the *muang* – the royalty and nobility, administrators, Chinese and Vietnamese traders and high-ranking royal military – were decimated due to emigration and socialist reeducation. Those "bourgeoisie" and aristocrats that stayed or failed to escape in time were sent to reeducation camps. An estimated sixty thousand of them died from hunger, disease or other causes (Kremmer 1997).

In the absence of capital and labor, the communist party planned to move directly from a peasant economy to socialism by destroying the remnants of "feudalism" and grouping peasants into collectives. Grant Evans (1990) describes the grotesque results of this forced conversion from subsistence ethics to col-lectivization in some detail. Wherever peasants were not forced into collectives, these disappeared immediately and peasants returned to their conventional style of subsistence agriculture (Bourdet 2000: 39). As early as 1979, the communist party admitted that collectivization was a failure.

Collectivization did not leave a great impression on local social structures. It was, however, accompanied by the extension of the communist party organization into the last corners of Laos. This was a significant change. The party was a new institution that now gained national relevance. The population was controlled by an all-encompassing party organization that reached practically every village. Laos became a fully integrated nation-state for the first time, something the French and the Americans had not been able to accomplish. The loose *baan-muang* structure was increasingly superseded by the nation-state.

Apart from peasants, small *muang* groups formed the population of socialist Laos. These were first all of those urban dwellers who had become communists. Interestingly, the precolonial structure – comprising an elite, a small group of city dwellers and the peasantry along with the Buddhist order – was reproduced under the surface of an egalitarian socialist state with a peasant economy. Of course, the *muang* groups were very small and most foreigners were gone. The dominant class now consisted of party leaders. Some of them had been peasants, laborers or employees before, while others had been members of the presocialist elites. The urban middle class, which had grown significantly during US intervention, was depleted.

Capitalist transformation

When Gorbachev announced the end of economic aid in November 1985, the communist party of Laos was forced to introduce changes. The small economy that had been financed by foreign countries for a century was now to stand on its own two feet. The party congress in November 1986 officially endorsed the introduction of a market economy under the title "New Economic Mechanism". After the Soviet Union pulled out of Southeast Asia, the Lao PDR found a new source of assistance, namely the international community. External forces and the dominant class of Laos now pursue the same goal, the development of a national market, especially by alluring international capital. Aid organizations, international organizations, and a few private investors are assisting the communist party in constructing a textbook Western society, from local workshops on irrigation to the use of fiscal instruments. While the economy follows the model of Western nation-states, the political sphere still follows the socialist model. As far as technocratic thinking is concerned, capitalism in the economy and socialism in politics get along fine.

The social structure of Laos is changing rapidly but the precapitalist sociocultures persist and still inform the majority of structures and habitus. The tendencies associated with the capitalist transformation are depicted in Figure 3.2. Subsistence peasants who do not remain peasants either become commercial farmers or agricultural laborers or they migrate into the towns. The small *muang* group transforms into the typical Westernized urban middle class

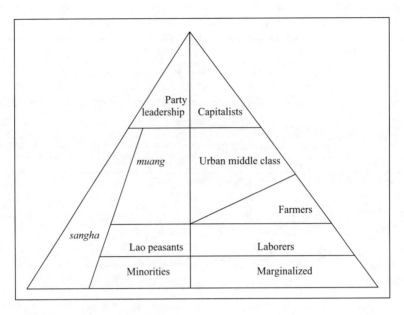

Figure 3.2 Capitalist transformation

comprising administrators, employees and civil servants. The *muang* and the socialist elites begin to engage in business and become capitalists. Chinese and Vietnamese reappear – partly in their colonial role as businesspeople but also as farmers, laborers and petty traders.

Some of the changes within the social structure are immediate consequences of technocratic development policies. Under the heading "eradication of poverty until 2020", the government (with active support from aid organizations) moves upland villages into the valleys, prohibits swidden cultivation, resettles small villages near marketplaces and improves the infrastructure. Population clusters emerge, which are increasingly well connected by road. The clustering also implies an ethnic mix with a significant pressure on ethnic minorities to adapt to the official culture and language, which are Lao.

The capitalist market develops in the towns, especially in the capital, Vientiane. Dwelling in a town, near the Thai border or near an important road means integration into the capitalist socioculture (Sisouphanthong and Taillard 2000: 147). In the countryside, plane and fertile land with access to water is still a considerable resource as well (Epprecht et al. 2008). It leads to commercial agriculture and production for the market only in those locations that are linked to the infrastructure to the degree that transportation of produce becomes economically viable.

Max Weber (2011) has associated capitalism with a particular type of rationality. Even if people spend their everyday life in a capitalist framework, it does not mean that they adopt a Weberian rationality. Many Laotians retain a precapitalist habitus. Almost half of the population has little to do with capitalism anyway. This segment was raised with subsistence ethics and continues to practice subsistence farming. These people are not untouched by socialism and capitalism but their primary habitus was shaped by subsistence ethics. Their economic life consists of growing rice, gathering additional foods and materials and managing to survive on the basis of the natural environment. Their social organization is dominated by the personal social structure. They have little to sell and to buy, nothing to invest as economic capital and rare contacts with the money economy.

A good example would be a peasant we interviewed in a remote village set in a beautiful mountain valley. He explicitly acknowledged the beauty of the place and argued that he would not want to leave because of this. He added that he had everything he needed and more. In town, people might have access to technology and consumer goods but not to clean air, quiet and nature. "We have lived here for generations. Our ancestors have chosen this place because it is auspicious. I know that the government considers us poor and backward but I do not think it is possible to find a better place." No economic rationality appears in the interview, because the interviewee does not see the world through this lens.

Even many townspeople still resist Weberian rationality. Ninety-five percent of the enterprises in Laos have fewer than ten employees. Typically, these would be relatives, members of the household or unpaid workers. They live in patrimonial conditions not conducive to the emergence of capitalist rationalism. The majority of enterprises actually are shops run by a family. Over the years, they develop economic planning and accounting but no serious idea of linking investment to profit maximization. Laborers and new urban middle classes develop a capitalist rationality but these groups are small. Laborers with a stable job and a decent income as well as employees do develop a capitalist habitus. They constitute the core of the new urban middle class.

Part of the patrimonial elite has returned to Laos, whereas another faction had stayed all along. The members of this elite and their offspring have learned to invest economic capital with the goal of profit. So have most members of the socialist elite. The usual arrangement is that one family member is active in the party, while others engage in capitalism. Patrimonial and socialist elites increasingly intermarry. Chinese, Vietnamese and successful first-generation businesspeople complement this group of capitalists, which incorporates capitalist culture and its patterns of action.

According to the census (National Statistical Center of Laos 2006), a little less than half of the population, or about 2.8 million, was considered economically active in 2005. Roughly 26 percent or 1.5 million were below the age of 11 years and 24 percent or 1.4 million were classified as inactive (students, retired and housewives or men who stay home and do the household). Of the economically active population, 64.3 percent were exclusively working in agriculture, while 21.5 percent did not pursue any agricultural activity. The remainder mixed agricultural and nonagricultural work. The census listed a total of around 320,000 employees, including civil servants and laborers, and 7,210 employers. The remainder of the total population, more than 2.4 million persons, were classified as "own account" and "unpaid family members". These comprise all subsistence peasants, many commercial farmers and all family businesses. Most commercial farmers and poor migrant laborers stay rooted in subsistence ethics. A lot of family businesses and former nobility retain a *phu-yai* culture. Many traders and employees develop hybrids of precapitalist and capitalist habitus traits. This leaves us with possibly 5 percent of the population as immediate candidates for a Weberian ethos.

Classes and milieus

In spite of the persistence of earlier biocultures and precapitalist habitus, the capitalist socioculture evolves. This entails not only cultural and ethical aspects but also the emergence of the capitalist class structure and its mode of repro-duction, which we have studied in the preceding chapter. We can observe its emergence in Laos. As Laos has become a capitalist society, albeit with a socialist form of government, an increasing number of citizens are distributed into classes and classified accordingly, even if they retain a precapitalist habitus and form of life. As explained above, capitalist classes develop out of precapitalist biocultures. As long as these persist, society is differentiated into rather dis-similar milieus; milieus being the intersection of biocultures and hierarchies (cf. Chapter 1 and Figure 3.3). We can distinguish the *baan-muang*, the socialist

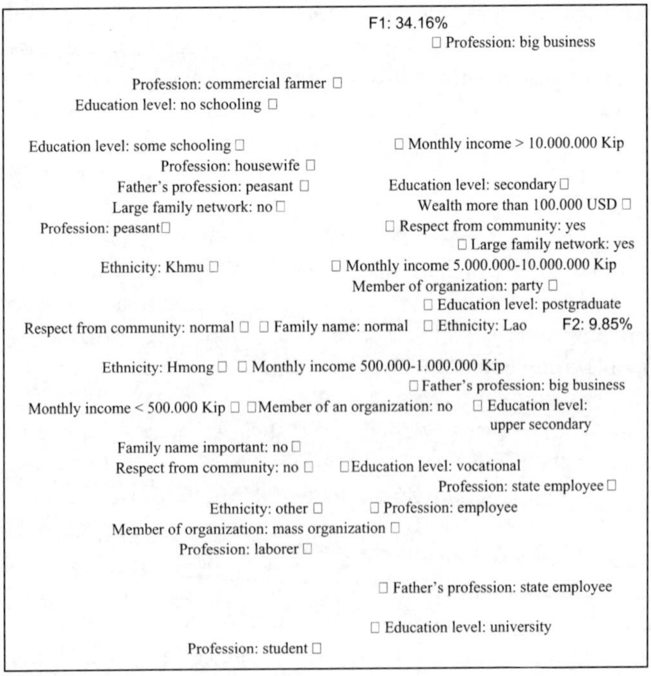

Figure 3.3 Multiple correspondence analysis (MCA) of biocultures in Laos

and the capitalist socioculture. Within the first, there is a hierarchy of ethnic minorities outside the structure, peasants in a difficult environment (often indicated by slash-and-burn agriculture and weak infrastructure), comfortable *baan*, urban *muang* population and nobility. Within the socialist socioculture, there is a hierarchy of ranks: village cadres, administration, leading cadres and party leadership. The capitalist hierarchy comprises the marginalized class (unemployed, beggars, day laborers), the working class, commercial farmers and traders, the new urban middle class and the capitalists. We will use the term "new urban middle class" to distinguish it from commercial farmers, the middle ranks of the party and the *muang* groups (cf. Chapter 5 for the new Indian middle class).

This class structure differs from countries with a longer capitalist past, such as Germany and Brazil. The new urban middle class in Laos mainly comprises professional groups that would be much better off in other countries and that would form an elite or an upper-middle class. In contrast, a petty bourgeoisie or middle class of the Western type does not really exist in Laos (yet). Its place is taken by the commercial farmers and traders, who in turn do not really form significant groups, let alone a class, in other countries. Finally, the other four classes are much smaller in Laos than in Germany.

Classes are rooted in tradition lines, which are divided into sociocultures. Each tradition line forms a segment in successive sociocultures. Very few members of ethnic minorities become capitalists or leading administrators and almost no former member of the nobility becomes a beggar or wage laborer. The younger generations tend to remain on the same level of the hierarchy as their parents even if they grow into a new socioculture. Therefore, they also share significant habitus traits with members of the former generation, namely their parents, often more than with another hierarchical level in the same socioculture.

Figure 3.3 shows the result of a multiple correspondence analysis with socially important characteristics carried out on the basis of our quantitative survey. We can discern nine clusters that correspond to eight of the milieus outlined above. The *muang* milieus and the middle socialist milieu are not visible in the figure. The reason is that very few members of those milieus are left. An additional cluster in our survey is formed by the students. In a way, they can actually be regarded as a separate milieu, as their way of life has a certain style of its own. However, they will not remain students for a very long time and merge with the capitalist classes. Therefore, we do not treat students as a separate milieu. Interestingly, the students' habitus closely resembles that of the neighboring cluster, the state employees (including teachers and professors).

The eight milieus apparent in our MCA (Figure 3.3) are summarized in Table 3.1. We see the non-*muang* milieu on the lower left both in the table and in the MCA, and the subsistence peasants above them. The commercial farmers appear in the capitalist socioculture in the table but at the top toward the left, just above the subsistence peasants, in the MCA. That is because most

Table 3.1 Milieus in contemporary Laos

Dominant class		
Patrimonial elites	Party cadres	Urban middle class
		Commercial farmers
Peasants	Rural party	Laborers
Minorities		Marginalized

of their characteristics have more in common with the peasants than with the urban population. Just below the center of the MCA are the laborers, to the upper right of them the employees and in the very upper right corner the capitalists. This is the capitalist socioculture. On the very right, starting from the bottom end of the y-axis, are the students, the state employees (including administrators) and the party elite (just below the capitalists). That is the socialist socioculture. It is further removed from the peasant milieus than the capitalist socioculture because the capitalist socioculture shares more with the two others than they share with one another. This may be surprising but will be explained further on.

We found that the majority of Laotians remain in the professional group of their parents, just as in Germany. In contemporary Laos, the fathers of most peasants today were peasants themselves, while almost half of the state employees had a father who was a state employee. Only one father in our sample was a businessman – and his son became a businessman as well. The same tendency to reproduce the family's social position is visible in education. If the father had been a member of the higher urban milieus, his children would inevitably have a high level of education. Out of our quantitative sample, only six respondents in this group had not completed lower secondary school. Almost all those who had primary education or less were children with a rural or lower class background.

If we add the correlation of people's profession with their paternal grandfather's profession, the reproduction of the social position and the impact of the social transformations become even clearer. Of the peasants and commercial farmers in our sample, only five persons (2 percent within these groups) report that their grandfather had not been a peasant or farmer. In contrast, where the grandfather had been a private employee, a trader, businessperson or administrator, none of our respondents had become a peasant or a farmer. They rather tended, as in any other society, to remain in the same professional group. Interestingly, the fathers of the two unemployed persons in our sample were a poor peasant and a factory worker. This clearly hints at the reproduction of the social position. We only see a significant differentiation if the grandfather had been a peasant or farmer. Even if the majority of the respondents were peasants and farmers as well, a large percentage had a different profession. This is a result of the social transformations.

Due to rapid capitalist transformation, Laotians change their livelihoods and transform their social milieus. By and large, we can say that people migrate from the left in Table 3.4 to the right, both physically and socially, while remaining in the same row or level of the social hierarchy. Marginalized peasants, especially from ethnic minorities, become unskilled laborers or beggars. Subsistence peasants with good land become commercial farmers; those with relatively poor land may become laborers. The *muang* groups have become the new middle class. The Vietnamese have returned as petty traders and entrepreneurs, whereas the Chinese have returned as businesspeople. However, Vietnamese, and especially Chinese, have also been immigrating as settlers and laborers.

If we now look at the individual milieus, their distinctness clearly emerges. The ethnolinguistic minorities have been on the margins of the *muang* and of colonial society. They participated in the independence struggle and some of them managed to move into the socialist leadership. But the vast majority have remained distant from the centers of power and capitalism. As they have had poorer starting conditions in the capitalist transformation, their relative subordination even partly increases. Among those claiming to own wealth worth more than USD 100,000 in our sample, forty-one are Lao, four are Hmong, one is Khmu and one is Chinese. According to the census of 2005, literacy among the ethnic Lao was 85 percent, whereas it was as low as 10 percent for the Lahu, 15 for the Tri or the Akha and 44 for the Lamet, some of the ethnolinguistic groups dwelling in remote mountain areas (National Statistical Center 2006).

Most members of the ethnolinguistic minorities remain subsistence peasants. As they tend to live in areas with little land suitable for commercial agriculture, they usually become integrated into the capitalist socioculture only when migrating to urban areas or abroad. Due to their low level of cultural and social capital, they end up as unskilled laborers, sometimes unemployed and sometimes informally employed. They lack influential family members and mostly any helpful social relations in the towns. Therefore, it is difficult for them to find employment in an economy that remains largely patrimonial and family-based. The formal sector is tiny and jobs for unskilled laborers very badly paid.

An example would be a Khmu we interviewed. He was born in 1985 in a remote village in Northeastern Laos. Thinking of his childhood, he recalls being hungry quite often, which he attributes to the fact that there was too little water around the village to grow a sufficient amount of food. Another important memory of his childhood is a violent father: "He beat me up on any occasion". The interviewee completed elementary school across the border in Vietnam, as it was the school closest to his village. He migrated to Vientiane by himself and not having any relatives there, he slept in the monastery. He managed to get a job as an unskilled construction worker and has remained in this field. In his spare time, he stays home and "sometimes" drinks booze. "I have no money to go out." His only wish is that his child will have a better life than he does.

Poor peasants, regardless of their ethnicity, seem unable to turn to commercial farming. This is related to the small size and bad quality of their land as well as to their lack of capital in general. Therefore, poverty is most widespread in the remote, mountainous areas. Even though this is not immediately related to ethnicity, these are the areas which are mainly settled by ethnolinguistic minorities. The quality of land, of course, is the main asset of the peasant, while market access and know-how are additional assets for the commercial farmer.

Many peasants lose their land to big extraction companies, agro-industry or rich landowners. Hannah Arendt (1958) has argued that the transformation of land into property is the core of the capitalist transformation, as it turns many peasants into landless persons who have nothing except their body, which they are to sell as laborers. In Laos, the expropriation of peasants is complex and occurs on several fronts. The French and the Americans started to turn land into property but did not get very far. Socialism, at least in principle, converted land into common or, more precisely, state property. Since the introduction of capitalism, international advisors have assisted the government of Laos in the process of land registration, which amounts to the commodification of land. The consequence is that poor peasants, people in immediate need of money and others are selling their land and turning themselves into potential laborers. Land is increasingly concentrated in a few hands, just as in any other capitalist transformation.

The registration of land has not been easy in Laos against the background of peasant society and socialism. The *baan* used to distribute their land before each season. Even if each household had its conventional claims to particular rice fields, they were renegotiated every year. This was done at village meetings that could last several days. In short, the immediate compound of the household was its property and was passed on to the next generation.

Population increase, improved infrastructure, the growing need to pay for goods and services in money, the legal registration of land and the belief of an easier life in the city lead to the typical migration of the country population. In other words, push and pull factors combine to drain the countryside of its physically most capable group. In today's remote villages, the age group of 15 to 40 years accounts for only about 25 percent of the population. A sizable proportion of migrants end up in slave labor or prostitution. Those who have relatives in town are in the best position. They often get some training or education or work in a family business. Almost all of the beggars in town are migrants without family. And most of the poorly paid untrained factory workers are recruited from this group as well.

Subsistence peasants with good land either remain peasants or turn into commercial farmers. The transformation can be incited by several factors: active development policy by the state or aid organizations, existing or emerging links to a market, a regular surplus in production or personal decision. The latter two factors usually only appear in peasants, who had been comparatively wealthy before the transformation. An existing link to the market also implies a stronger integration before the transformation.

The former *muang* population largely disappeared from Laos after 1975. Very few have stayed and some have returned. They now occupy the same positions and often have the same professions as they did prior to 1975. As the economy is no longer colonial or quasi-colonial but formally capitalist, they are formal entrepreneurs or employees now. Their habitus is rooted in the *phu-yai* culture but decades living abroad or under socialism have transformed them. Very few real *phu yai* are left, as demonstrated by the MCA (see Figure 3.3).

A woman we interviewed was an interesting example of someone rooted in the *muang* structure, even though she was only born in 1955. Her father was a highly educated man and for a period of time occupied a high position of employment working for the state. He sent her to the best school in Vientiane and to high school in Australia. She then went to language school in Australia but returned to Vientiane, because her high social position was not being acknowledged and she experienced racism in Australia. But soon after her return in 1973 the family fled to France after selling most of their property. She began working in a luxury hotel in France, studied management and married a Frenchman. Later, she obtained a PhD. She is about to return to Laos and move into one of the properties that her family still owns. Instead of retiring, she wishes to help educate the Laotian population and to advise the government.

The communist party continues to exist. Even though less than 3 percent of the population are party members, its influence reaches into every village. Village heads are supposed to be members, even if not all of them are. Many state employees are members as well, which assures the party a large degree of control over the population, via its administration. Furthermore, many businesspeople are party members, either to facilitate their business or because they used their membership to set up businesses. Finally, the party has made use of the Buddhist order as an organ of information and control. Important monks are often party members.

Membership in the party opens many doors and works as social capital. However, the party has an internal hierarchy, which means that not all ranks open up the same possibilities. A rural village head usually remains a peasant or becomes a farmer. In one of the villages we studied we interviewed the village head. In his 40s, he became village head. In spite of his position, he states that "we are very poor". In monetary terms, this is certainly the case, as his family earns about USD 30 per month. At two hectares, he has enough land, however. He claims to have no hopes for the immediate future except subsistence.

The situation is different for urban party members. This is illustrated by a retired government employee. His father was a soldier and he himself joined the revolutionary party in 1961. He received education in Vietnam and after 1975 additional training in the Soviet Union. Upon his return, he held an important position in the Ministry of Defense and briefly took up an even higher post at the provincial level before retiring in 2005. His wife was a government employee as well, and so are his children, and all of them are party members. They lead a comfortable life even though they are not rich.

Just as socialism had to be adapted to the local peasant society, so it has to adapt to capitalism today. In urban environments, a very peculiar blend of socialism and capitalism emerges. The milieus concerned are the intermediate party ranks and the new urban middle class. In some cases, they coexist in the same person, in others, they are strongly opposed to each other. A substantial percentage of educated Laotians are very explicit in their anticapitalism, inspired both by subsistence ethics and by socialism. But all of them have been affected by the capitalist socioculture in their everyday life, even state and party administrators.

The dominant class in any capitalist society mainly consists of heirs of pre-capitalist rulers and nobility. The same is true for Laos. Many names of dominant class families under colonial rule appear in the contemporary dominant class. As in any other capitalist society, some of those names have disappeared and new ones have been added. And similar to many capitalist countries, this is due to a revolution in which prominent members of the earlier regime were replaced by revolutionaries. In the case of Laos, however, this was a socialist revolution. Therefore, the contemporary dominant class comprises members of the old *muang* elites, the socialist leadership and capitalists. The three groups increasingly merge through intermarriage and they become more and more capitalist in habitus and ethos.

This process of an emerging dominant class is very similar to what has happened in other capitalist nation-states. We see the alliance between political (revolutionary) elite, capitalists and old nobility as the drivers of the capitalist transformation from seventeenth-century England to nineteenth-century Germany to twentieth-century South Asia. The dominant class of Laos differs from many others in two regards, however. First, it is very small, which means that virtually every member is somehow related to everyone else. Second, its members mostly still have a job – as a party leader, running a business or even in the military or administration. Other dominant classes are characterized by the fact that they do not have to labor, as we have seen with regard to Germany. If anyone has wage-labor in these societies, he or she does so in order to administer the wealth or out of personal motivation.

The precapitalist sociocultural milieus slowly transform into capitalist milieus and thereby into classes. The new classes are heirs of precapitalist ranks and continue to transmit their heritage to the next generation. The transmission establishes tradition lines that have their origins in precolonial times and survived several significant transformations in Laos. In view of the capitalist hierarchy, the heritage consists of habitus and capital. Their transmission from one generation to the next increasingly stabilizes the hierarchy of classes and reproduces the relative social positions.

In Laos, there are two typical deviations from this general tendency. First, the revolution did lead to social mobility. The pattern of mobility is easily explained. All those who actively participated in the revolution, irrespective of social background, had the chance to become officials after 1975. Children from educated households and those revolutionaries who received further training abroad became high officials and party leaders. The second type of social mobility is actual migration from peasant households. Here the pattern is rather typical as well. Those with family networks in the city had the chance to move upward and become small self-employed businesspeople, skilled laborers or employees in the private sector, while those without family become unskilled laborers, monks or remain otherwise poor. The first type of mobility took place between 1975 and 1995; the second type still persists, even though upward mobility is decreasing.

If we take a closer look at the rich Laotians in our sample, defined as people with wealth worth more than USD 100,000, we see that one third of their parents were peasants, one third state employees and the remainder mainly businesspeople and presocialist elites. Even though the group of the rich extends far beyond the layer of the dominant class, its composition has its roots in all three or, rather, four sociocultures: *baan*, *muang*, socialism and capitalism. This would not have been possible without the socialist and the capitalist transformations and the ensuing social mobility.

Our MCAs for Laos show that a large amount of one type of capital is mostly accompanied by large amounts of other types of capital. In Figure 3.3, we see concentrations of capital on the right half, and we see where it is lacking on the left. Cultural capital is concentrated on the upper right, and symbolic capital on the lower right, while the x-axis basically corresponds to the amount of economic capital. In contrast to Northatlantic countries, such as Germany, the correlation between social position and cultural capital is not very strong in Laos, even though it clearly exists and is becoming more prominent. This is similar in Brazil and India. Of those individuals with less than secondary school education, only 7 percent earn more than USD 300 per month, whereas 14 percent of the respondents in our sample with at least secondary schooling earn more. Four percent of the respondents with less than secondary schooling have wealth worth more than USD 100,000 as opposed to 9 percent in the group with at least secondary schooling. In other words, secondary and tertiary education double one's chances of accumulating economic capital.

Chances increase with the level of education but many capitalists in Laos do not have a tertiary degree and many of those with a degree, such as teachers and professors, earn low salaries. Employees in Laos who are comparatively well educated feel that they earn too little. Education derives its value less and less from a possible career in the political field. To a certain degree, all education accomplished before 1989 has been devalued. Only studies in economically important areas – especially English, business and some technical subjects – have an increasing value.

In contrast, social and symbolic capital are very important in Laos. Bourdieu has seriously underestimated their value also in Western countries, as we have argued in the preceding chapter. However, in Laos their value partly reflects the persistence of precapitalist sociocultures. *Baan, muang* and socialism attribute a higher value to social factors than to economic capital. This is reflected in the fact that respondents with wealth worth more than USD 100,000 are twice as likely to be members of the communist party than those with less wealth. They also have a higher likelihood of participating in a mass organization. Sixty percent of the wealthy report to have a large family network as opposed to 26 percent of the less wealthy. Only 2 percent of the wealthy think they do not have a large family network. Of course, these numbers are probably exaggerated, since we asked for a self-assessment. But they can still be used as indicators of the value of social capital in contemporary Laos.

A similar connection exists between wealth and symbolic capital. Whereas 43 percent of the respondents with wealth worth more than USD 100,000 claim their family name is very important and well known, only 14 percent of the less wealthy do so. Even more striking is the correlation between wealth and respect. None of the wealthy think that they receive little or no respect from the community, while 75 percent believe they do. In contrast, only 40 percent of the less wealthy claim to receive respect from the community. Of course, it remains unclear whether family name and respect are the consequence or the root of wealth. Therefore, it cannot be established whether or not this symbolic capital is anchored in precapitalist sociocultures. However, it is likely that a high social position in a precapitalist socioculture goes hand-in-hand with social and symbolic esteem that can be used as a resource in the capitalist socioculture.

The value of economic capital in capitalism is evident. Most goods and services are commodified and have to be paid for. This is clearly demonstrated by the fact that 82 percent of our respondents with a reported monthly income of less than USD 50 state that they do not have enough in terms of goods, whereas only 18 percent of those with an income of more than USD 1,000 say the same. However, income and wealth alone cannot determine the social position even in a purely capitalist society. Without symbolic and social capital, economic capital opens up many opportunities but is not sufficient for upward social mobility. Think of attitudes toward the *nouveaux riches* or successful sport stars who are not being allowed into the inner circles of the dominant class.

Habitus groups

Initially, we applied the methodological approach developed in Germany to our study of Laos. In the course of our research, however, we realized that the construction of binary "elementary categories" only makes sense when studying a stable social structure. Even though we did find binary oppositions useful in interpreting the empirical material from Laos as well, they do not take the historical dimension into account. Therefore, we combined the search for habitus categories with the study of social change in Laos in order to anchor the roots of each habitus in a socioculture and to trace its further development in particular social environments.

The categories useful for discerning habitus groups in Laos are probably rooted in the historical tradition lines and acquired in early childhood. We defined these in discussions related to our qualitative interviews. The interpretation was performed together with a group of professors at the National University of Laos between 2010 and 2013. On the basis of the interpretations, the questionnaires for the final sample of qualitative and quantitative interviews that are the empirical foundation of this chapter were developed and applied.

In the quantitative survey, which was used to construct the following habitus types, the main characteristics extracted from the qualitative interviews were used in questions asking for self-assessments in the form of yes-or-no questions, oppositions and graded comparisons. Of course, self-assessments in question-naires are far from reliable. However, given a sufficient number of responses, they can hint at tendencies. This is exactly what this interpretation does. It does not claim to offer a precise reconstruction of quantifiable and clearly defined habitus types, but tendencies. The interpretation is not random because it is anchored in qualitative work and theoretical considerations.

Four large habitus groups emerge from our MCA of habitus traits. The first cluster could be called the depressed habitus type, the second cluster traditional-ist, the third disciplined and the fourth ambitious. The first cluster is characterized by lack: of self-determination, of self-confidence and of satisfaction. The second is defined by traditionalism, community-orientation, dissatisfaction and a lack of goal-orientation. The third cluster comprises the traits of self-determination, discipline and self-orientation. The final cluster is characterized by goal-orientation, an experimental attitude to life, satisfaction and an interest in power, career and ambition. These characteristics appear in Figure 3.4, which corresponds to Figure 2.10 in the chapter on Germany. The correlation between the factors is not as clear, since it also expresses the heterogeneity of sociocultures, which is no longer visible in Germany.

The characteristic of self-determination can be interpreted as the main distinc-tion between upper and lower levels in the social hierarchy, whereas traditionalism

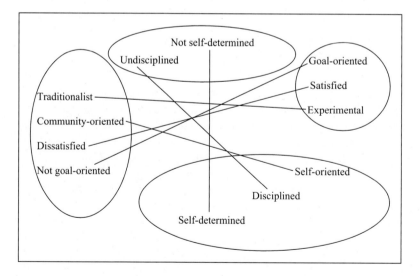

Figure 3.4 Proximity and distance of habitus traits

and community-orientation distinguish the *baan-muang* socioculture from capitalism. We have found the characteristic of self-determination, or autonomy, to be the marker of upper classes (and its lack or absence to be the marker of lower classes) in Brazil and Germany as well. It may be a general attribute distinguishing upper from lower classes in capitalist societies. For this reason, it has been depicted as the y-axis in Figure 3.4. The horizontal characteristics, in contrast, are specific for Laos and rooted in the diocultures. In principle, the characteristics on the left are linked to the *baan-muang* socioculture and those on the right to capitalism. Traditionalism and community-orientation are core traits of the peasants, while discipline and self-orientation characterize capitalism.

We would have expected a correspondence of habitus groups with sociocultural milieus and more differentiation of the capitalist habitus types. It seems unlikely that all Laotians should be reduced to four types. However, we have to consider that almost everybody who was born between about 1965 and 1985 grew up as a peasant, and that this is even true for the majority of those born before and after. This entire group, certainly the majority of the population, can be reduced to one habitus type. The life forms of the ethnolinguistic groups are very diverse but they share subsistence ethics and personal social structure as well as some principles of action, which are incorporated in the habitus. Apart from that, the differences between these groups are dwarfed by the differences between them and the new urban middle class. This is the point of the habitus construction.

Even more surprising is the lack of any specifically socialist habitus type. This issue was already alluded to on page 66. Contemporary socialist milieus seem to absorb some characteristics of the capitalist socioculture. In fact, pure apparatchiks are hard to find in contemporary Laos. Still, a more subtle analysis will reveal a differentiation of the disciplined and the ambitious habitus types into a socialist and a capitalist version with some distinct core characteristics. At the same time, both types share the same history to a large degree, as they have emerged out of the same tradition lines, with the few exceptions of the exiled *muang* population.

The depressed habitus type, broadly speaking, comprises the marginalized groups of the *baan* and capitalism. The traditionalist habitus is incorporated by all the others who are rooted in the *baan-muang* socioculture. The disciplined type is found among the population that is firmly integrated into the socialist and/or capitalist socioculture. The ambitious type characterizes the upper echelons of Laotian society.

The depressed habitus type is characterized by negative attributes, that is, by a lack of traits that are valued in society. We found a similar type, also characterized by lack, in Brazil and Germany: the fatalistic type. This type also lacks exactly the same traits: autonomy, goal-orientation, discipline and self-confidence. We decided to call the type in Laos depressed because it has been oppressed and is linked to a feeling of exclusion and marginalization. It prevails in the social environments most removed from the centers of power. This habitus type comprises up to 30 percent of the population in Brazil and about 10 percent in Germany. The percentage in Laos would be closer to the German figure.

The core trait of this habitus type is the lack of initiative, which is not due to a psychological deficiency but to continuous marginalization. Due to the poverty of the parents and their often remote location, representatives of this habitus rarely receive much schooling and have to help their parents in agriculture and household chores at an early age. No professional training is added to the poor educational background. As members of a marginalized family, they never accumulated many relevant social ties and social respect, which could be transformed into social and symbolic capital. The depressed social situation during the formation of the habitus results in low self-esteem, which in turn appears as a lack of initiative, self-determination and goal-orientation.

The depressed habitus is incorporated by those without any serious opportunities in society. This translates into a lack of land in the rural environment and a lack of capital (in Bourdieu's sense) in the towns. It is likely that this group was significant under colonial rule but almost disappeared in socialism. It comprises a high proportion of ethnolinguistic minorities and almost exclusively descendants of poor peasants: unskilled workers, unemployed, beggars, rural laborers and marginalized peasants.

This type is exemplified by a peasant from a Mon-Khmer group who lives in a Lao village. He is the only person without land in the village and practices slash-and-burn cultivation on the slopes of the nearby mountain. The other villagers consider him to be poor. During a village festival, he is invited to join the party after the members of the village "establishment" have finished eating – I watched him eat all the leftovers. He is about 74 years old, in poor health and still has to work every day. His son helps him but could not feed the family alone. Another son went to Vientiane looking for a job but reportedly makes less than USD 50 a month. None of the family members has completed elementary school.

The reader unfamiliar with Laos might have suspected that this type only appears among the lowest class in urban environments. This is not the case. Basically every village hosts at least one poor family without land or a tiny stretch of rugged terrain. Since the land registration, the rural population has become more unequal. Besides, the entire population of Laos has been integrated into the nation-state and into global capitalism. There are, as a consequence, entire villages that are classified as poor and targeted by special development programs. They become objectively and subjectively marginalized.

The traditionalist habitus type is mainly composed of all those socialized in the *baan* or *muang*. The characteristic of traditionalism expresses this. Almost half of the population still lives in this socioculture and significantly more have been raised in it. Therefore, the traditionalist is by far the largest habitus type. Apart from traditionalism, it comprises community-orientation and a lack of goal-orientation. These characteristics are evidently part of subsistence ethics. They are also the direct opposites of the traits embodied by the new urban elites, even if some members of these elites have their roots in a peasant environment.

The fourth characteristic of the traditionalist habitus type, namely dissatisfaction, also places it in opposition to the urban elites and in proximity to the depressed type. The peasant was the hero of the revolution and now is the epitome of underdevelopment. All peasants are aware of this and seriously frustrated about it. More generally, this habitus type is unhappy about the shift to capitalism and the associated problems, such as individualism, competition, alienation, environmental degradation, corruption and crime. All of these issues were presented as problems of contemporary society not only by peasants but also by traditionalist urbanites. However, the characteristic of dissatisfaction must not be overrated. The majority of traditionalists are satisfied with their life – but not to the same degree and in the same proportion as the elites.

This habitus type shares lack of goal-orientation with the depressed type, whereas the two other types are goal-oriented. The meaning of this differs slightly between the types, however. The depressed are not goal-oriented because they have hardly any opportunity to set any goal. The traditionalists do not have any goals within the socialist or capitalist sociocultures but they do pursue the goal of subsistence with diligence, planning and devotion. They also strive for plenty of other goals, such as having a nice garden, weaving beautiful textiles, brewing effective booze or making pleasant music. These are possibly more meaningful goals than making money or climbing a step on the career ladder but they do not lead to an improvement in social position or "merit". This is the framework that defines a goal in a capitalist society.

An emphasis on the community instead of the self is another important component of subsistence ethics. This includes reciprocity, a communal ontology and sense of identity, cherishing personal relations and togetherness, a sense of duty and mutual help. On this basis, the *baan* not only secures survival but also creates its specific form of life. The associated values and patterns of behavior are transplanted into urban environments by those who have found a position in the state apparatus or the capitalist economy, which is the majority of the urban population born before the 1990s.

Basically, any peasant habitus is an example of the traditionalist type. Once the peasant has found a suitable environment, change is a threat. Under the present conditions, traditionalism transforms from security into a backward-oriented attitude. One peasant, whose village is doomed because of resettlement, says: "Our present location is perfect. We have enough to eat, the weather here is just excellent, it could not be better elsewhere. Now we have to move together with people from other villages closer to town. The soil there is not as good. I have no idea how we can survive there." It sounds a bit like paradise lost.

In Chapter 1 we have argued that the disciplined habitus is typical for capitalist societies. It characterizes the lower and intermediate middle classes, who have to perform wage labor to make a living without attaching much meaning to their jobs. In Laos, this habitus type is also characterized by an orientation toward the self as opposed to the community and by a significant degree of autonomy. It is incorporated mostly by the new middle class and the socialist administration as well as commercial farmers and laborers in favorable conditions. The disciplined habitus in Laos deviates from other capitalist countries in two ways. First, it also extends to socialist milieus. Second, it extends beyond the lower middle class.

In terms of discipline in Foucault's sense, socialism does not differ much from capitalism. An individual is supposed to perform wage labor and his or her social value is determined by this. In fact, the laborer is the hero of socialism even more than he is of capitalism. The ideal is the fully disciplined and homogeneous society administered by a technocratic party leadership. While the population did not comply with this program in Laos, the administrators themselves did. Within this framework, they incorporated a disciplined habitus, which is useful in the capitalist socioculture to a similar degree.

Apart from discipline, self- and goal-orientation characterize this habitus type. The emphasis on the self instead of the community opposes this type to the traditionalist and expresses the specific individualism of capitalism. This does not mean that each person is singular, but somewhat egotistic. In fact, Lao peasants are pretty individualistic in terms of their personality compared with Westerners (cf. Chapter 1). Self-orientation means that survival depends on individual activity. The meaning of goal-orientation is linked to this. The atomized individual in capitalism has to organize his or her own life. Some people lack the means to do so and tend to embody the depressed habitus type. Those who do have the means to organize their life-course can be classified as goal-oriented. In this sense, goal-orientation does not only distinguish the capitalist socioculture from *baan-muang* and socialism, but it also exists above the level of the marginalized.

The group of socialist administrators, including educators and government employees, is located in the social hierarchy of socialism beneath the party leadership. It is also part of the tradition line that transforms into the new urban middle class. In capitalist Laos, only the capitalists themselves are positioned above this class. In Western countries, a privileged class of functional elites stands between them. The new middle class of Laos is likely to transform into an elite over time. The disciplined habitus type is the most numerous after the traditionalist type and is bound to grow as capitalism spreads.

An extreme case of the disciplined habitus type is a tailor we interviewed. She was born in 1961 as a daughter of tailors in the remote South of Laos. Her parents taught her how to sew. She married a man who turned out to be a drunk and adulterer, and so she filed for a divorce after her son was born in the year 2000. As the sole breadwinner, she built up a tailor shop and makes up to USD 1,000 per month. She uses much of this to send her son to Japan to get a good education. The tailor reports that she has been working so much that her health has become affected. Therefore, she has started to give sewing classes, which she intends to make her sole profession in the future.

The ambitious habitus type is typical for the elites in all the countries we cover in this book. It incorporates the values and symbols of capitalism but is restricted to the upper classes. The type shares goal-orientation with the disciplined type but differs from it in its means and goals. Whereas the middle classes are characterized by discipline and a certain modesty, the upper classes strive for more. The middle classes have alienated jobs to survive and are content with a comfortable lifestyle but the upper classes seek positions of power, creative and influential jobs, self-expression and more than a sufficient amount of material goods.

The ambitious habitus type is set apart by ambition and self-confidence. It strives for the top positions in society and has the means to do so. In any of the sociocultures of Laos, ambition makes sense only to those in the upper echelons of society. The bulk of the population has no possibility to move up in society. Within the *baan-muang* socioculture, people are tied to their lot by their symbolic rank and their form of life. Within the socialist framework, mobility is possible, but the upper ranks have been reserved for the dominant groups since the revolution. In capitalism, the types of capital we discuss in this book are required for social mobility.

Therefore, ambition is linked to self-confidence. Whoever is born into a powerful family and has the means "to do anything" develops an outstanding self-confidence. It is interesting that people in leading positions in all the societies we have studied consider themselves a species apart from the rest of the population. While they claim to have reached their position due to ambition and merit, they explain their success by their outstanding abilities. This, of course, reconfirms their self-confidence.

This habitus type also comprises an experimental attitude to life, as opposed to traditionalism. Change, challenges and new problems are the norm, not the exception, and require new solutions. Climbing the social ladder also poses new challenges and creates changes in the way of life. In this sense, an experimental attitude is the prerequisite and the consequence of a habitus equipped for this type of environment. Of course, leaders are conservative in many regards but they do not live in the stable environment of the peasant, who best follows the recipes developed by previous generations in cooperation with the community. "Experimental" is supposed to refer to the social attitude, not so much to excitement in everyday life or scientific quest.

Certainly, the ambitious habitus type characterizes many members of the dominant class but it also occurs in the new urban middle class and among commercial farmers. One example is a man who works for the central committee of the communist party. He is a member of a very small ethnolinguistic minority. Even though he grew up in a remote area, some of his elder family members had joined the revolution and became members of the party elite. They made sure that he got a job with the party as well. "I already have a university degree but now I want to get my Master's in order to qualify for higher positions. . . . I am married to a Lao. She is a party member as well. We have a very good family network and are devoted to the cause of socialism."

In many respects, the socialist attitude to life corresponds to that of capitalism: discipline, labor and productivity as core values, a belief in science, a formal egalitarianism and even, to a certain degree, the myth of meritocracy. In these regards, socialism is well prepared for the capitalist socioculture. It differs from the capitalist habitus in its emphasis on solidarity, the critique of social inequality (which goes beyond formal egalitarianism) and the strong integration of the party and the state. The socialist habitus in Laos has mainly developed in a peasant culture, which is reflected in its particular interpretation of solidarity, equality and even the state.

It is significant that habitus, ethos and satisfaction with life in general correlate in Laos to a certain degree. It comes as no surprise that 100 percent of the capitalists in our sample claim to be "very satisfied" with their lives, while 100 percent of the unemployed are "dissatisfied". More surprising is the fact that only 28.5 percent of peasants report to be very satisfied with their lives. A closer analysis reveals that these are mostly Lao, whereas the less satisfied groups comprise a high percentage of ethnic minorities. Likewise, merely 30.8 percent of the petty traders and 25.7 percent of the laborers claim to be very satisfied. These groups are, together with the unemployed, those that are integrated into capitalism as the lower classes.

The "spirit of capitalism" is closely related to the capitalist ethos but it comprises capitalists, elites and laborers alike. On the one hand, there are those who have learned to play the game of capital investment and have the means to play it. On the other hand, there are the groups that have to seek wage employment in order to make a living. The laborers clearly consist of two groups, those that have a choice and live a comparatively autonomous and affluent life and those who have to take any job at any pay.

Gender inequality

Gender inequality is as relevant for Laos as for other countries. And similar to Germany, each socioculture and class has its particular version of it. Increasingly, class becomes more important than gender but in most contexts, gender and class combine to favor or devaluate a person in several dimensions (cf. Crenshaw 1989). In a Lao village, men and women complement each other but are not equal. In our survey, all men and most women claimed that the male was the household head. Miao-Yao are much more patriarchal than Tai-Kadai and Mon-Khmer. In a Lao village, the husband is supposed to move in with the wife's family, the youngest daughter to inherit the house and the woman to run the household. However, real practice often differs from these principles (Lao Women's Union 2000: 18). Land is supposed to be split among the children but the registration of land usually results in legal ownership of the land by a male child (Lao Women's Union 2000: 32). Women do usually run the household, go to the market and organize petty trade.

The *muang* was clearly dominated by men. All monarchs were men except Nang Maha Tewi, who ruled for ten years in the fifteenth century. However, so many monstrous legends refer to her that it is uncertain whether she ever existed (Ngaosyvathn 1995: 24). All important functions in the administration and the entire *sangha* were staffed by men. This tendency was certainly strength-ened under the French, who did not even consider the existing matrilocality and matrilinearity as a legitimate possibility of inheritance.

On an ideological level, socialism demands equal rights not only for all classes but also for all genders. In practice, however, socialist policies in Laos were ambivalent. The communist party called for gender equality and many forms of inequality were actually combatted, such as discriminating language, prostitu-tion, and female beautification. At the same time, it defined the "three virtues" of Laotian woman as being a good citizen, good mother and good wife (Ngao-syvathn 1995: 60). Especially on the level of party positions, women were marginalized to the same degree as under the Royal Lao Government (Khouang-vichit 2010: 52). Both aspects were important to define gender relations in socialist Laos. These aspects as well as village and *muang* gender relations persist but are being transformed.

Women continue to dominate petty trade and were quicker to grasp immedi-ate opportunities of the capitalist market economy. Small enterprises, microcredit institutions and markets have been dominated by women. In contrast, women are often marginalized in the formal sector. They earn less for the same job and are often employed without pay. Formally, all citizens are equal in a capitalist society and everybody has the same economic opportunities. Women, however, tend to have less capital than men, including symbolic capital. They also continue to be responsible for children and the household, which are time-consuming yet unpaid activities. Inequality in the political realm continues as well, even though the leadership actively pushes gender mainstreaming. Still, between 2006 and 2010, only 1.3 percent of the village heads, 2 percent of the district gov-ernors, 8 percent of the ministers and no provincial governors were female (Khouangvichit 2010: 57). In the capitalist socioculture, gender is increasingly shaped by class.

Carol Ireson (1996: 197) has summarized the characteristics that are neces-sary for women to succeed in the market economy: access to markets, education, Lao language, ability to work in factories. All of these characteristics are gener-ated by class and not by gender, but they are distributed differentially between women and men within the classes as well. Furthermore, globalized gender stereotypes and relations influence the younger generations in Laos. They do not aim at gender equality but reinforce the image of the strong man and the beautiful woman, which prevails in the other countries we study in this book.

Conclusion

This chapter tried to demonstrate how capitalist transformation leads to the emergence of classes, using Laos as a case study. We found that the classes emerge out of segments in earlier hierarchies and form tradition lines. The earlier hierarchies persist to some degree but are being transformed. In a few decades, they will be hardly visible any more, as is the case in contemporary Germany or Brazil. On the level of habitus, however, the persistence of earlier sociocultures is likely to endure for several generations, as important components of the habitus are transmitted in the family by the elders, who grew up under precapitalist conditions and incorporated a noncapitalist habitus. We have argued that this is true for the overwhelming majority of Laotians alive today.

Lao society is much more heterogeneous than Germany, as it is undergoing a rapid capitalist transformation. This entails a persistence of precapitalist habitus forms and hierarchies. The transformation also leads to a different class structure. We discern five classes in Laos, instead of four in Germany. The classes also have different roots and are even linked to different segments of the division of labor. However, the mechanisms producing and reproducing social inequality within the emerging order of classes are the same as in Germany. The following chapter on Brazil will take a closer look at these mechanisms and the dividing lines between classes.

Notes

1 This chapter is based on Rehbein (2017). Material from this book is used by permission.
2 The research team in Laos had a total of around 40 members, very few of whom contributed consistently. The team was led by Kabmanivanh Phouxay. Core members were Vilaythieng Sisouvong, Suvanny, Udone Vongsommy.
3 We will use the term "Laotian" to refer to the citizens of Laos and the term "Lao" to refer to the ethnolinguistic group speaking Lao as its first language.

4 Understanding the class struggle in Brazil

In Brazil, the existence of social classes is evident even to the casual observer. The connection between contemporary classes and the colonial order of the past, based on slavery, is also evident. Finally, the connection between class structure and recent political events in Brazil is acknowledged by most commentators. The question remains, however, about the precise definition of classes. In order to explain the contemporary political struggles in Brazil, one has to understand recent transformations in the class structure of Brazilian society. In view of this goal, it is important to reconstruct the recent socioeconomic process that enabled the social ascension of tens of millions of Brazilians. The recent political struggles are related to this.

Brazil, like Germany, has a long history of capitalism and a solid class structure. Like Laos, and in contrast to Germany, it was constructed by colonial rule. Contrary to India and Laos, not the entire population was declared equal upon gaining independence, as slaves, women and ethnic minorities only gained full citizenship over time. These inequalities have persisted until today and inform the Brazilian social structure. In these regards, Brazil has more in common with the US than with India, even though it shares many structural features of inequality with South Asia.

In Brazil, we can draw on decades of empirical research on social inequality. For this book, we have conducted six hundred qualitative life-course interviews of the same type we have used in the other countries.[1] The sample is representative of the Brazilian population in terms of income class, sex, federal state and ascribed race. For the interpretation that forms the foundation of this chapter, we selected 108 interviews. We discussed and encoded each interview in a group that consisted mainly of Brazilians. Finally, we applied multiple correspondence and regression analyses to the data.

The chapter first establishes a description of the class order in Brazil and looks at the classes in more detail, focusing on the distribution of capital. The second section studies the classes more closely in terms of their everyday life and incorporation of the habitus. The main part of the chapter is devoted to the reproduction and legitimation of the dividing lines between the classes. The dividing lines have already been referred to in the preceding chapters. This chapter discusses them in more detail and links them to an incorporated classification and its moral legitimation as well as to the current political situation. We argue that incorporated classification lies at the root of social inequality. This argument unfolds in the following chapter on India and is revisited in the final chapter.

Social classes and capital

Understanding the actions of social classes is a hard task, because of the received wisdom, which is based on the interests of those who are, and strive to remain, in power. Making social class invisible is the principal need of every discourse of power. The reason is simple: the opening up of the class perspective enables the criticism of all the unjust privileges that literally unfold from the cradle to the grave. This is the deep reason behind all the misunderstandings about the definition of what determines social class. The first misunderstanding is the confusion created by economics, that social class is defined by income level (liberal economics) or by place in the scheme of production and occupation (Marxist economics). Despite committing the same mistake, that of the unilateral perception of the world (explaining people's behavior solely by economic factors), the two forms of economics are certainly not identical or interchangeable.

Public discourse in and on Brazil readily uses the term "class", albeit in a certain sense. The existence of entrenched inequality is hardly questioned (Kühn and Souza 2006). However, the liberal foundation of the discourse persists and serves to mask the actual structure and reproduction of inequality. In Brazil, classes are defined as income levels A, B, C, D and E, corresponding to multiples of the official minimum salary (*salário mínimo*: sm). The "brilliant" idea behind this division is that the differential behavior between individuals is produced by the amount of money made. Thus, though they are all the same from the start, individuals in class A are supposed to behave differently from individuals of class E because they have a greater capacity to consume than the former.

The assumption, therefore, is that these individuals share the same world view and the same capacities, being differentiated only by a purchasing power so miraculously unequal. As no word is said about the hidden genesis of these differences, the field is open to meritocratic explanations that disguise the social construction of all individual privilege. To all intents and purposes, the individuals from class A are diligent workers, and the individuals from class E are lazy and stupid. In the recent Brazilian debate about the notion of the "new middle class" (Pochmann 2012), the bankruptcy of this definition of class becomes even more obvious: middle class becomes class C, as they are at the median level of the income scale. This is pseudoscience serving as the disinformation of the general public.

In the preceding chapters, we have pointed to the fact that social class is a socio-emotional construction which happens from birth within the family. Not all families are the same, as each social class has a distinct pattern of family socialization, and later on these differences in family socialization of belonging to a certain class determine access to the labor market with distinct levels of income. An upper income reflects a family socialization in the corresponding class, first at school and later in the labor market. Here, as almost always, obscuring the genesis of social processes serves the political interest of making the causes of inequality and social injustice invisible. Social classes, and their study, are fundamental as they allow clarification of the best-kept secret of modern societies: the fact that they are not societies of individuals competing under conditions of equal opportunity, but rather societies that perpetuate unjust class privileges.

In the recent period of social ascension of the lower classes in Brazil, we have seen examples of strong and sometimes violent reactions of the established middle class to the process of social ascension of the lower classes, which was interpreted by many as an electoral ploy of stupid and lazy poor people. As the reconstruction of this process of "class struggle" in Brazil in the last 15 years is fundamental to understanding recent political events, we shall look at this movement in two steps: first, we reconstruct the idea of social class and demonstrate its fundamental importance in understanding society; then, we analyze the opaque manner in which solidarity and prejudice between classes are constructed and how we can make them visible.

Effective understanding of the world requires reconstruction of the concept of social class. Without it, we cannot understand how the world works and how we have become victims of manipulation by the lowest of the media. How does Brazil work as a society of classes in struggle for scarce resources? What is the relationship between the classes? What conflicts and alliances are possible between them? Who exploits, and who is exploited or manipulated?

The seemingly fundamental fact of life in a capitalist society is competition for the scarcity of all resources. Even if there is the possibility of alliances and of solidarity between individuals, the fact of competition between everybody and against everybody, and of the potential conflict that this competition sets up, is the essential starting point. The competition is not only about the possession of material goods such as fridges, cars and houses, but also in regard to the relationship of possession of nonmaterial goods such as prestige, recognition, beauty, charm, admiration, etc. We all fight with everything we have for the scarce material and nonmaterial resources that are our deepest desires and our dreams, whether waking or sleeping.

As we are born into an actual family, none of us come out of limbo or from the clouds, but always within a context of history and of a past already built for our family heritage. It is because of this that the histories of individuals are, without exception, premolded by the family prehistory. And it is also because of this that we can only understand individuals if we understand their early family history, as there is no abstract "family" but each social class has a very specific family socialization, as we have argued in the preceding chapters. All the chances of individuals in the competition of social life depend on their class origin, transmitted through their family socialization.

When we talk of "capitalism" or of "modern society", we want to differentiate the kind of society we are referring to from other types of society, with other types of needs of continuity. In capitalism, social reproduction depends on the amount of inherited and acquired capital in Pierre Bourdieu's sense (see Chapter 1). Economic capital is easy to understand, because capitalism is about economic capital. However, capitalism does not work and does not reproduce itself properly without "useful knowledge", which constitutes cultural capital. There is no function either in the market or in the state that can be fulfilled without accumulated knowledge. Because of this, the privileged classes are the classes that monopolize economic and cultural capital, always unjustly, as their privilege is transmitted from birth, which is not chosen. As this heritage is always within the family, whether it be economic and therefore more visible, or cultural and thus less visible, social class will always determine all the chances of success or failure for any individual in the world. The terms of family and social class already point to the third type of relevant capital, which is the social capital of important relations one can draw on.

Our hypothesis is that modern Brazil is composed of four main social classes: (1) the dominant class, i.e., the tiny group with money, materially exploiting and symbolically dominating all the others; (2) the middle class and its various segments, which mirror all the forms of individuality that the ownership of valued cultural capital entails, and which has to perform all the work of social domination done in the name of the moneyed. In the end, it is the middle class judges who judge, teachers who teach, journalists who write and, in general, all those who occupy the intermediary positions between the dominant moneyed elite and the majority of society who have no privileges: (3) a working class of fighters (batalhadores), who lead a precarious life; and finally (4) the class of the excluded, which we provocatively call the "unworthy Brazilians" (ralé estrutural) – a class which, as we shall see, is situated below the line of "dignity".

On the basis of our data, it is not possible to give an estimate of the relative proportions of each class, as the sample was not representative of the Brazilian population. It is likely, however, that the ralé estrutural comprises up to 40 percent of the population, the batalhadores amount to maybe 30 percent, the middle class accounts for another 25 percent or so and the dominant class comprises only a tiny fraction of the Brazilian population. The percentages are entirely hypothetical and serve the purpose of giving a very rough idea of the proportions.

The classes differ greatly in their characteristics. We can almost define class and establish class membership on the basis of one single characteristic alone. For example, most members of the ralé estrutural have no wealth, batalhadores little wealth, members of the middle class a medium level of wealth and those of the dominant class excessive wealth. A few members of each class may differ from the rest in their wealth – while resembling them in all, or almost all, other characteristics. For example, the "black sheep of the family" in the dominant class may have been disinherited but would still share all other characteristics with his father, while a member of the ralé estrutural may have won the lottery but will most likely lose all of this money during his lifetime. Therefore, it is necessary to consider the characteristics in their combination and as statistical

Table 4.1 Classes and their characteristics

	Ralé estrutural	*Batalhadores*	*Middle class*	*Dominant*
Income	0–1 SM	1–2 SM	2–40 SM	40+ SM
Wealth	none	little	medium-high	very high
Educational title	none or low	médio	superior	superior
Social networks	irrelevant	irrelevant	relevant	very relevant
Occupation	none, informal	many, informal	skilled	capitalist
Childhood	tough	medium	easy	easy
Education in the family	not stimulating, violent/distant	somewhat stimulating, not violent	stimulating and close	stimulating
Self-confidence	0–1	0–1	2–5	5
Autonomy	0–1	0–1	3–4	5
Active attitude	0–2	0–2	2–5	5
Intellectualism	0	2	4	5
Idealism	1	2	2–3	1
Satisfaction	0–1	1–2	4	5

values. Still, any Brazilian shares the overwhelming majority of the characteristics listed in Table 4.1 with the other members of his or her class. Some of the correlations between the classes and single characteristics are summarized in the tables throughout this section of the chapter.

Table 4.1 lists those indicators that distinguish the classes from each other and the characteristics that are shared with a high likelihood by all members of the class. We established the indicators on the basis of our qualitative interviews. For this reason, these were the indicators that were used for the MCA establishing classes in Brazil. The indicator for education listed in the table actually joins two that were used in the data interpretation, while the indicator on profession in the table is more general than the concrete answers given by the interviewees. Of course, all of the indicators in the table are also used to define class, which seems to imply a circular argument. However, as the correlation between class and the values of the indicators is statistical, it could be very weak. The stronger the correlation is in statistical terms, the more likely class is actually determined to some degree by this particular indicator. The values for the indicators in the table are typical ones for each class.

We use income and wealth as indicators to measure economic capital. Income is defined by the *salário mínimo* (sm), wealth is estimated and includes housing, car(s), and financial assets. The educational title refers merely to the highest formal level attained and does not include the school type or location. Social networks are weighed according to their reach and relevance on the basis of the interview interpretation. For occupation, the official Brazilian codes are used and then grouped according to the classification of four occupational classes by Oesch (2006).

Two of our indicators refer to childhood in order to assess the roots of the primary habitus. The main objective of these indicators is to find out to which degree the person has been supported during childhood. This includes emotional, social and intellectual support. The interpretation looks at factors like violence, distance and stimulation. These factors are combined to form an indicator. The self-assessment that the interviewee gives of his or her childhood complements the evaluation quantifying the degree to which the person experienced the childhood as easy.

A list of core habitus traits is added: self-confidence, autonomy, an active attitude to life, idealism, and an emphasis on the intellect. In order to assess the value of each indicator, it was correlated with its opposite and asked which side of the dichotomy was stronger. Self-confidence is the incorporated attitude that one can master all problems in life and is on the right track. It is opposed to insecurity. Autonomy refers to the embodied level of choice: does one feel that one is free to do what one wants? It is opposed to heteronomy. Idealism refers to higher, society-oriented and sometimes unrealistic goals, whereas the opposite, pragmatism, is an attitude that focuses on a realistic relation between given means and attainable goals. Intellectualism refers to the prevalence of intellectual activity in life, as opposed to physical activity.

After establishing the indicators, we encoded the interviews by attributing each indicator values on scales from −5 to +5. The resulting dataset was fed into a multiple correspondence analysis, which neatly distributed the four classes to the four quadrants of the graph. Each class is characterized by a cluster of indicator values that are traits of capital and habitus. Since the Brazilian habitus types are very much linked to class and almost entirely correspond to class lines, the following section will focus on the distribution of capital to the classes.

It is almost self-evident that income and wealth are indicators for class membership. If we look at wealth distribution in the sample, it becomes clear to which degree the classes differ in this regard – and that it is almost an indicator of class itself. Table 4.2 shows the correlation between class and wealth. It is

Table 4.2 Class and wealth

Wealth:	Dominant class	Middle class	Batalhadores	Ralé estrutural
Very high	100%	18%	0%	0%
High	0%	47%	0%	0%
Medium	0%	45%	33%	0%
Low	0%	6%	57%	47%
Very low	0%	0%	10%	53%
Total	100%	100%	100%	100%

easy to see that not a single member of the two lower classes has more than medium wealth and that no member of the two upper classes has less than high wealth. In terms of percentages, 100 percent of the members of the dominant class have very high wealth, 73 percent of the middle class have medium or high wealth, 57 percent of the batalhadores have low wealth and 53 percent of the ralé estrutural have very low/no wealth.

In terms of income, the distribution is similarly clear. *All* the members of the dominant class have an income above 40 *salários mínimos* (sm), almost all members of the upper middle class between 20 and 40 sm (with one earning less and one more), most members of the lower segments of the middle class between 5 and 20 sm, most batalhadores between 2 and 5 sm and *all* members of the ralé estrutural a maximum of 2 sm (except one who earns just a little bit more). As with wealth, the extreme classes are very distinct and defined, with the middle classes having some overlap.

Table 4.3 shows the relation between class and social capital. As it is very difficult to measure social capital, the interviews were interpreted in view of the degree to which the interviewees claim to have drawn on networks in their life-course. Has a family member assisted them financially? Has a friend helped them find a job? Was it possible to escape a legal case because of good connections? Questions like these were addressed to the interviewee. Then the interpreters had to assess the value of the social networks used according to an ordinal scale with five levels. The result is that all the members of the dominant class and most members of the middle class have very important networks, while 63 percent of the ralé estrutural and 46 percent of the batalhadores have irrelevant or almost irrelevant networks.

A similar correlation emerges with regard to the background of social capital, which is developed during childhood. If you grow up in an affluent neighborhood and attend an elite school, your friends are likely to occupy important positions in society as adults. Therefore, the social environment during childhood can be used as an indicator of social capital. This was assessed similarly to the

Table 4.3 Class and networks

Importance of networks:	Dominant class	Middle class	Batalhadores	Ralé estrutural
Very high	100%	45%	13%	5%
High	0%	34%	23%	21%
Medium	0%	11%	18%	10%
Low	0%	6%	46%	42%
Very low	0%	3%	0%	21%
Total	100%	100%	100%	100%

Table 4.4 Class and education

Highest level:	Dominant class	Middle class	Batalhadores	Ralé estrutural
No schooling	0%	0%	0%	6%
Fundamental	0%	0%	18%	74%
Medium	0%	0%	38%	20%
Superior	100%	100%	44%	0%
Total	100%	100%	100%	100%

importance of social networks by interpreting the interviews and encoding them on a five-level scale. The result is that all members of the dominant class lived in a high or very high social environment during childhood, a total of around 90 percent of the middle class in a medium or high environment, 74 percent of the batalhadores and 95 percent of the ralé estrutural in a low or very low environment. In this dimension, the batalhadores resemble the ralé estrutural more than the middle class. The reason is that historically they have a similar social origin and are rooted in the same social class of the last century.

In the dimension of cultural capital, the differences between the classes are very significant but only in terms of an exclusion of the lower classes. As Table 4.4 shows, all members of the two highest classes have attended and most often completed their high school, which is the level of a superior completo. No member of the ralé estrutural has even attended high school, while not even half of the batalhadores have attended or even completed high school. This also shows the great importance of education in the upwardly mobile class of the batalhadores in opposition to the ralé estrutural. The figures in the table do not distinguish between incomplete attendance and completion of the level with a title.

As far as habitus is concerned, some of its traits are very much linked to class, while other traits differ within classes. The three characteristics that define the extremes of Brazilian society to the highest degree are self-confidence, autonomy and an active attitude to life. These characteristics are relevant in Germany and to a lesser degree in Laos as well. *All* the members of the dominant class in Brazil in the sample are very self-confident, autonomous and active (except for one person who is only medium autonomous). On the other hand, almost 70 percent of the ralé estrutural are insecure or very insecure, around 60 percent are heteronomous or very heteronomous, and only 35 percent show a significant degree of activity in their habitus. We interpret these characteristics as rooted in early childhood and as elements of the primary habitus. They are fundamental traits of the personality and cannot be modified easily in later life. They partly determine our options and goals. Therefore, they are very important for "success" or "failure" in society.

The incorporation of class

Even the moneyed need some cultural capital to be accepted in their group. Without it, the access to the social capital of important relationships is shaky. An uneducated rich "savage" cannot make any alliances with important peers, nor a profitable marriage, to increase the capital accumulated. At least some overlap in taste and behavior is necessary, even though the role of high culture in Brazil (and Laos) is much less pronounced than in Bourdieu's (1984) France. Building some cultural capital of "distinction" in relation to the other classes to show that money is not the mark of their lifestyle, but rather that it is the fruit of a supposed innate good taste, is also vital for the dominant class. The right to property, which is the foundation of economic capital, is transmitted by inheritance and by marriages which are supposed to increase their wealth, and not fragment it. Business deals with their peers also require this social capital, which only the mix of money with some form of cultural capital can offer.

The inverse happens with the middle class in its various kinds. Although its privilege is based on incorporation of cultural capital, some economic capital is necessary so that they can buy, for example, free time with their children. Unlike the children of the lower classes, who have to study and work from adolescence onwards – which almost always implies doing neither one nor the other well – the children of the middle class can dedicate themselves just to studies. This allows them to concentrate on the more highly valued cultural capital for the employment market, which they will enter later on. This basic fact is overlooked when defining social classes by means of external attributes such as income.

In fact, human beings are formed as such by internalization, or rather, by the unconscious or prereflexive incorporation of forms of behavior from the parents or people who perform these functions – that is, those who care for children and who are thereby loved by them. The most important relationship of the socialization process of any human being is therefore primarily emotionally affective. In short, we are what we are because we imitate those we love. Children "incorporate" their parents in silence and invisibly – who has not enjoyed watching a child of two or three walking beside the father with the same sway of the body? – and this is the most relevant fact for us to understand the reproduction of the social classes over time.

If economic capital is transmitted by inheritance and property titles, cultural capital is transmitted by an invisible inheritance, which requires that the inheritors have the same emotional and affective structure that enables the correct inheritance of the social position and its incorporated characteristics (Bourdieu 1984). This inheritance may include curious facts, such as the father's way of walking and speaking, but also includes other aspects that determine success or failure in social life. An example of the latter is the capacity to concentrate in school, which is a specific privilege of the middle class. Family generations receive the baton from the previous one and specialize in creating all the right conditions so that they are "winners" first in school and then in the labor market. There is a bond, almost never perceived, whether in received wisdom or in the official social sciences, which links family socialization to school and to the labor market.

With these bonds being forged during family socialization, in the family home and at a tender age, they are not thought of as privilege. It is for this reason that the middle class becomes the class par excellence that believes in the meritocracy. As most of the stimuli are incorporated unconsciously during childhood socialization, it is as if they had been born with them. An illusion is thus created of merit being individually attained, rather than determined by the family and social environment. While middle-class children play with toys that stimulate their creativity, hear stories from the mother full of fantasy that stimulate their imagination and see the father reading every day (stimulating their liking for and perceived importance of reading), the everyday experience of the lower classes is very different.

The son of a construction worker plays with his father's wheelbarrow and learns to be an unqualified manual laborer. He perceives his mother's praise for schooling as lip service, since the mother's schooling has helped her little or not at all. It is above all the example lived that constructs children of different classes as winners or as losers when they enter school at the age of five. Because of this, understanding the different family socializations between the classes is so important. Without it, we do not realize privilege acting as it most likes to act, that is in silence and invisibly, and we reproduce all kinds of prejudice as if there were people who chose to be poor and humiliated.

In the lower classes, the distinction between laborers and the excluded – which is quite fluid, as we have seen in recent years of politically engineered social inclusion – becomes one of degree and not of quality. Poor Brazilian families are not just poor, and their misery is not just economic. They reproduce an everyday life of cognitive want which tends to prolong the moral and affective misery, due to the centuries of abandonment by a socially irresponsible slave-owning society. Even in the families that are still able to maintain the family model of a loving father and mother taking care of the children as well as possible in adverse circumstances, the parents are only able to transmit their own social maladaptation. One cannot, after all, teach what one has not learned. We see mothers worried about their children's schooling, but as they know that school has made no difference to their own lives, they do not effectively perceive and teach how it can make any difference in their children's lives.

When we interviewed adult members of the ralé estrutural about their school experience (Souza 2009), we were surprised about the generalized affirmation that they had "spent many hours on end without learning". The "capacity of concentration", which enables learning, is not a natural given of any "normal" human being, like having two eyes, a mouth and two ears. Without stimulation to read and without reading as a part of everyday life, there is no "capacity of concentration". Without capacity to concentrate, in turn, there is no real learning, and it becomes intelligible why the state schools for the poor largely churn out functional illiterates. Worse still, in our interviews, the poor socialized in this precarious schooling of precarious pupils felt guilty for their supposed "innate stupidity". Imagine having had the chance of going to school and not having taken advantage of it. The cycle of domination is closed when the victims of abandonment see themselves as the cause of their own misfortune.

But there is no condemned class. Favorable conditions and the "political will" enabled countless numbers of the "unworthy", the long-term excluded with no chance of redemption, to make the climb up to legalized employment and to unprecedented chances of consumption. Furthermore, some of them also had the chance to attend quality technical schools and even state and private universities on account of virtuous policies of social inclusion. It is access to valued cultural capital that effectively changes the life of people. Many of them climbed out of the excluded class and became batalhadores, albeit still in precarious jobs, in the competitive economic market.

The dividing line between the two lower classes reflects the possibility of differential appropriation of what we call "cultural capital". Although the cultural capital at play here is not highly valued by the middle classes, any labor under the conditions of competitive capitalism requires incorporation of knowledge. More than that, as we saw in the example of the middle classes, there is no incorporation of knowledge possible without the prerequirements of relative educational success being fulfilled. The fluid line between the working class and the excluded class is constructed by the greater or lesser possibility of incorporation of the affective and emotional prerequirements that enable the avoidance of complete educational failure. What separates the laborer from the excluded is that he or she is able to incorporate a minimum amount of knowledge useful in the competitive market. With family socialization and schooling a bond is produced that afterwards enables the selling of what was learned beyond muscular energy and physical strength.

The definition of useful labor produced through knowledge or through "manual effort" (not very different in this sense from animal power) is fluid. Formal jobs, as construction worker or sugar cane cutter, are in reality, a mixture of the two dimensions. Even so, it is possible to separate the types of family socialization by social class – whether it enables or disables one to learn at school and afterwards to exercise productive functions in the competitive labor market. None of us are born with the attributes of discipline, of prospective thought and the capacity of concentration. These attributes are privileges of class. Some classes have them "from birth", such as the middle class; others construct them precariously, like our working class; and others still never construct them in any suitable amount, like our population of the excluded.

In summary, we can briefly describe the four classes on the basis of their capital and habitus. The ralé estrutural is characterized by negativity. Its members lack most of the capital and habitus traits that are relevant to attain any higher function, social status and respect in contemporary Brazil. Even their patterns of action are defined by lack. They lack self-confidence, an active attitude and autonomy. Their only traits that can be defined positively are an orientation toward the body and hedonism – but these characterize only one habitus type of this class. They lack the means to lead a life considered decent by society.

For this reason, the other classes do not treat them with dignity (Souza 2007). In all our interviews with members of the higher classes, contempt for the lowest class is evident. Furthermore, the ralé estrutural is characterized by little goal-orientation and by a strong tendency toward traditionalism. It is not a revolutionary or an experimental class. The class is mainly divided into two habitus groups, one of which is idealistic, passive and insecure, while the other is body-oriented, hedonistic and much less insecure. It is interesting to observe that no family of any member of the ralé estrutural in the sample was intact and stable. All parents were divorced or separated and very few of the interviewees had a stable relationship themselves.

The batalhadores are people who are rooted in the ralé estrutural but were upwardly mobile due to changing circumstances. Social programs in Brazil and new job opportunities in the low-paid service sector combined to offer jobs in the grey zones of the economy to people who lack everything except the determination to leave the ralé. This determination is reflected in the relatively high values for the indicators of work ethos and appreciation of education. A strong determination is required to organize one's life under adverse conditions and without a trained habitus. The level of education is much higher among the batalhadores than among the ralé estrutural (cf. Table 4.4). Otherwise, the batalhadores live just above the line of dignity that separates them from the ralé, but this line is very porous. The more optimistic members of the ralé estrutural are moving into the ranks of the batalhadores, while the very passive, insecure and idealistic batalhadores have a strong overlap with the same habitus type in the ralé. The two main habitus types of the batalhadores are an experimental, intellectual and hedonistic one, while the other is more goal-oriented, traditional, autonomous and rather family-oriented. The income of this class is low but always comprises at least two salários mínimos.

The middle class differs strongly from the two lower classes because its members have incorporated all the characteristics that are necessary for a respected life in society: discipline, skills and a "life plan". Their childhood is structured and predisposes them for an organized life and a stable profession. Even if some families do not make more money than some families of the batalhadores, the stability and regularity of their jobs creates a completely different attitude to life and time (Stoll 2012). One can plan for the future and even for the future of one's children. This is reflected in the stability of the families, the high value and level of education, the stimulating atmosphere for children within the family and often a strong goal-orientation. The two habitus types that prevail within the middle class are an active, family-oriented, pragmatic and ascetic type and an experimental, hedonistic, self-oriented and idealistic type. They also cluster in two different generations, indicating a move toward family-orientation among the older generation.

The dominant class is mainly defined by an excess of wealth. In spite of that, many members of this class still have a job because the job often helped them make their money. There seem to be few wealthy families in Brazil that have to do as little as European noble families to sustain their position. However, the aloofness of this class even in Brazil is reflected in the fact that, on average, it has a lower educational title and a less pronounced work ethos than the upper middle class. In all other indicators, the dominant class tends to surpass the upper middle class despite all similarities. The economic and social capital of this class, especially, are in a league of their own and have nothing in common with the rest of the population.

Even though we encounter four classes in Germany and Brazil, their structure and size differ significantly from each other. This is due to their different pre-histories. While the two lower classes in Brazil have the same origin and both are rooted in precapitalist slavery, the middle class emerged from the white urban dwellers and the dominant class from the colonial landowners and over-lords. The two tradition lines of the German fighter class are the proletariat and the employees. Structurally, they have little connection to the marginalized class. The Brazilian structure reminds one more of the Lao structure, but on closer inspection this is only the case for the two upper classes in the capitalist socioculture and not so much for the rest. However, we will argue in the remainder of the chapter that a structure of four classes is a likely long-term result of the capitalist transformation.

The legitimation of social injustice

In the preceding section, we have tried to demonstrate that the classes are formed primarily by differential familial socialization enabling them, also differentially, to exercise the fundamental functions for the reproduction of capitalism as a system. It is the access to economic, cultural, social and symbolic capital that enables the reproduction of the system as a whole, both in the market and in the state, which constructs the hierarchy between the social classes. It also predetermines the chances of individuals to a large degree in the competition of everyone against everybody for scarce resources.

But we have not yet addressed the main issue. Capitalism pretends to be just. In the end, the most important moral justification of the modern world is that everyone has equal chances. How can one then justify such obscene inequality as we see in Brazil? Moreover, how can one understand the question of inequality, central as it is in modern societies, having been substituted by other ad hoc agendas constructed to make it secondary? To examine this point we have to recognize that capitalism sets up not only a hierarchy of classes but it also sets up a kind of very singular and historically unique legitimation and justification. But if there is a need to justify, it is because there is a "moral" backing of the system as a whole, as the central question of morality is to establish the distinction between the just and the unjust, and in capitalist societies justice is linked to the notion of "universality". As we shall see in greater detail, the vast majority of societies follow this principle. There is a whole complex juridical and contractual order designed precisely to show that people, so diversely apportioned by life by their belonging to a class, are treated as equal.

No doubt, in some countries, this universality and this equality are more successful. But in no society are they perfect. There is, therefore, in all capitalist societies, the production of invisible moral hierarchies that are very effective and active. Their practical effect anyone can perceive, with concrete examples from everyday life. It is these moral hierarchies – opaque and invisible but concrete to anyone to see in everyday life – that enable the unequal treatment of individuals due to their belonging to a class, counter to the logic of equality and of formal universality of the visible juridical order.

In the clearest English, capitalism claims to be egalitarian and fair, and because of this develops a complex of formal equalities that populate the constitution and all the legal codes and contracts of mandatory application. Because the perception of inequality and of real injustice created by the inequality of inheritance of class has to be suppressed, there comes into existence a hierarchy "felt" by everyone in his or her everyday life, but at the same time never addressed openly, never reflected on and never portrayed as a hierarchy. This is an effective hierarchy which rests on the origin of class, and not on formal equality under the law.

Even though this principle is valid for all capitalist societies, whether in the global South or the North, some societies have come closer to justice defined as equality and universality than others. The abyss between the real hierarchy and formal equality is much smaller in Northern Europe than in Brazil. Unlike the ridiculous and weak "inherited cultural belief systems" (da Matta 1981) with which we explain the difference between Brazil and the Northatlantic societies, the criterion of the greater or lesser difference between the dream of egalitarian justice and its practical realization is a much better instrument for measuring this distance, which is real.

The question is how the hierarchies are constructed and felt – and how do they build on inequality as the major principle in relation to the formal equality that everyone swears they pursue? And how do the opaque and hardly visible "other hierarchies" that are used to justify the class struggles of the privileged against the marginalized manage to remain opaque, without seeming to be a flagrant injustice and evil? These are the two most important questions we must address to understand the dynamic of the class struggle in contemporary Brazil. Without this discussion, the coup of 2016 is perceived as being the fruit of personal and localized action. Its fragmentary perception implies its noncomprehension.

We address these central questions in two stages. First, we try to show how contemporary capitalism constructs the invisible moral hierarchies that enable the repositioning of inequality as the foundation of a type of society which sells itself as being egalitarian and fair. Then we establish that, in the Brazilian case, we have further hierarchies which were constructed to channel class resentment and to exacerbate inequality even further.

Even if we are blind to it, there is a whole moral hierarchy in contemporary societies. However, in everyday life and in received wisdom, we only see the effect of money and power. It is because of this that classes are constructed on the basis of income, reducing our intelligence to the minimum and increasing our ignorance to the maximum. But money and power need to be legitimized in everyday life by moral standards, otherwise they cannot produce their effects. On the other hand, we also feel emotions we are unable to explain and that do not necessarily have anything to do with money and power – such as remorse, guilt, envy, resentment and admiration – which, to a large extent, explain our concrete actions in the world.

What "world" is this that mixes affections and emotions with moral hierarchies and that cannot be explained by action, nor money or power? Although we are blind to this important world as such, we are able to reconstruct it through actions and reactions that people make in the practical world. A well-designed and well-conducted empirical study can reconstruct the practical relevance of these moral hierarchies for our concrete behavior, although we are hardly ever conscious of the hierarchies. What we have in the head is much less important than the way in which we act and behave in practice. Normally, what we think we are is, to a large extent, the fruit of the need to justify and legitimize the life we lead. It does not necessarily reflect the "truth" of our behavior. As various critical thinkers have demonstrated, the primary need of human beings is not the truth. Far from it. Our primary affective need is to justify and legitimize the life we lead (Bellah et al. 1985). Mostly, this separation mirrors the distance that separates science from the ingenuous posture of received wisdom.

What is important here is to highlight that it is possible to demonstrate beyond any reasonable doubt the effect of these moral hierarchies or lines of social classification, despite being invisible in everyday life, where we perceive only the workings of money and of power. In fact, these moral hierarchies and these "moral sentiments" can be observed in their effects on the practical actions of people, even though "in our heads" we do not have the least idea of their existence. The fact that we are not conscious of the causes of the moral sentiments and the moral hierarchies which are their source only makes them stronger, for in this way we are unable to obtain the necessary reflexive distance from them.

The great French sociologist Pierre Bourdieu was a pioneer in demonstrating the influence of these invisible lines of social classification created by the moral hierarchies in modern society. In his most important work, *Distinction* (1984), Bourdieu was able to demonstrate that the exalted equality in republican France, based on quality state education for all, was a fiction. Not in the sense that the republican and egalitarian French effort was a failure – far from it. If we compare France with countries such as Brazil, we see that the effort was a great success. What Bourdieu demonstrated is that in spite of having set the standard for common "dignity" of all French people, a standard that does not exist in societies such as the Brazilian one, French society constructed, as an example to all other capitalist societies, alternative and subtle forms – which are hardly perceptible to anyone immersed in the perspective of everyday received wisdom – of justification and legitimation of inequality and privilege.

Bourdieu's classic work analyzes aesthetic taste as an invisible mechanism of producing social distinction, in the sense of legitimizing the perception of the superiority of some and the inferiority of others. It is the aesthetic taste that received wisdom imagines to be beyond discussion and that is said to be unique for each person, as in Immanuel Kant's "disinterested pleasure". Not only is taste not individual, but it is shared and constructed socially, and works as a form of invisible legitimation of all kinds of actual privilege.

Practical examples are easy to find. For people who drive expensive cars, wear fashionable clothes and drink special wines, this kind of consumption does not only mean that they have more money than others who cannot afford such things. More than anything else, it means that they have "good taste", which implies a superiority that is not just aesthetic but also moral. As we have seen, everything we associate with the spirit has a link to the divine, and nothing represents the spirit more than good aesthetic taste. Those who do not have it are perceived as mere bodies, having needs just like animals, and are therefore inferior in the aesthetic and moral senses.

Everyone who sees him- or herself as representative of the spirit develops a solidarity with peers and a prejudice against those who do not share this vision of the world. In fact, taste is not restricted to the isolated consumption; it develops into lifestyles that encompass the whole of social life. It is not just the expensive special wine, but also the kind of food people eat, the clothes they wear, the holidays they choose, the friends they cultivate etc., as Bourdieu (1984) has demonstrated in his work. These are shared lifestyles that give the feeling of superiority that cannot be bought, but has to be lived, thanks to a special taste and lifestyle that are a select privilege of a minority. The majority without such access suffers the prejudice – conscious or unconscious – of not just being poor in the economic sense, but also of not having "spirit", and therefore serving as an example of a degraded form of human existence.

These are invisible lines of social classification and disqualification based on moral hierarchies not perceptible in received wisdom – which imagines that power and money are the sources of all social hierarchies – that become the basis of solidarity and of prejudice in modern societies. We shall see how this point is decisive in understanding how the prejudices of the traditional middle class relate to the rise of the lower classes in the recent history of Brazil. For now, the important thing is to perceive distinction by good taste as a decisive element both in understanding the solidarity between those above, as well as understanding their prejudices in relation to those below (the lower classes). Although the distinction by taste is ubiquitous in society, it serves primarily to legitimize the differences and the privileges of the middle and high classes in relation to "the people".

This argument draws on the work of the Canadian philosopher Charles Taylor. Taylor is a pragmatic philosopher who does not restrict his research to the history of philosophy itself. Rather he is interested in ideas and the values that enabled ordinary men and women to acquire practical strength. These are important ideas and it is worth making the effort of reflection to understand their influence in our lives. Taylor (1989) has tried to show that in contemporary societies, two value-ideas control our lives: the notions of authenticity (or expressivity) and of dignity. Both reflect a process of learning, which is its moral dimension, and a process of distinction and legitimation of social domination, which represents its intercalation with the pragmatic dimensions of money and of power. In the end, every human action is intercalated in this double dimension that is both utilitarian and moral. What changes in each individual is the greater strength in relation to one aspect or the other.

The dimension of authenticity is more recent, historically speaking, and only in the twentieth century, especially in the context of the counterculture of the 1960s, did it reach a truly popular dimension. Before this it was something restricted to the alternative intellectual elites. Authenticity means the absorption in social life of the moral principle of the "sensitive human being" as the value-guide for practically leading one's life. The important thing is that this idea is not just to have money or power, but rather to live life in accordance with feelings and affections that are particular to each person, in a biography that is always quite individual.

The notion of "sensibility" comes to mean special attention to "reflected feelings", which are not to be confused with blind and animal passions. It is, in a manner of speaking, a sublimation and spiritualization of our affective dimension. Therein lies the relevance it came to take on from the eighteenth century onwards throughout the whole of Western, educated civilization, becoming widespread in this century. It is precisely this notion of "sensibility" that Bourdieu calls "good taste" as an invisible mechanism producing class solidarities and prejudices. However, Bourdieu does not perceive the possible learning that inhabits the sensibility as a moral dimension, seeing it solely as a producer of social distinction to oppress the lower classes. Taylor, in turn, does not see the potential effect of this principle to produce hierarchy and prejudice.

Our point is that it is both, the "possibility of learning" and the producer of "social distinction" to legitimize privileges. This principle becomes important when it is institutionalized in universities, museums, in the arts, as well as in its pastiche version in the modern cultural industry. The entire history of Western culture lives in the big box-office films, self-help books and best-selling novels, as well as Manicheistic soap operas. These products are not there to educate and stimulate critical thought but rather, to the contrary, merely to reproduce in conformist and stereotyped versions a sensibility to be readily sold. In this way, one does not have to consider that sensibility is only authentic if it is discovered and constructed individually through hard effort. However, the very success of this industry of pastiche and of filling out is only possible because the notion of sensibility has already taken hold of the popular imagination, even in those who have not constructed an authentic sensibility and are obliged to buy it. In this way, we can perceive the social efficacy of an idea, when it dominates us all, whether we want it or not, whether we perceive it or not.

The late historical construction of the notion of sensibility or of the sensitive human being takes place through opposition to the other great source of moral hierarchy in the West, which is the notion of the dignity of the useful producer. "Dignity" here is not to be confused with the imprecise notion we give it in received wisdom. This notion is much older and begins to be constructed with the Christian ethics of "control of desire and of the passions" by the spirit, being linked to the value notion of social respect as deriving from "productive work in favor of the common good", as Taylor (1989: 216–23) explains. As continued productive labor requires discipline and self-control, the idea of dignity in successive stages comes to be perceived as the capacity to discipline and control desires and passions that make discipline impossible.

The protestant revolution is yet another deepening of this line of progression in the sense of always requiring more control and discipline of work and of the worker. If Christian ethics in the broad sense construct the idea of the spirit as superior to the body and therefore the idea of having to control desire and the passions, then Protestantism makes labor "sacred", as Max Weber (2011) has argued. Labor becomes the path to God and to salvation in the other world. Although in the secular world reference to God is no longer obligatory, labor continues to be the principal reference of every individual through concretization of the abstract idea of God which is transformed into the idea more palpable as the "common good". The greater or lesser respect and admiration we give each other in society comes to depend on our performance in labor. Whether we like it or not, we admire people – even if we envy them – for their good performance on the job. This is concrete proof, which anyone can test in everyday life, of the strength of moral ideas that constrain us. It is as true in Brazil as it is in Germany and Laos.

This means that the source both of self-esteem of the individual in Western capitalism, and of the social respect due to it, is linked indelibly to useful labor. Just as we admire those who work well, we despise or feel pity for those who perform no useful labor, such as the work of parked-car keepers in the large Brazilian cities. Labor and sensibility are the two forms of moral hierarchy we know and practice, whether we are conscious of this hierarchy or not. In a capitalist society, the two most important dimensions in life, which define success or failure, are precisely those of labor and of emotional life.

It is an empirical verification of the validity and of the penetration of ideas proposed in this book, which anyone can do alone by reflecting about what really matters to them. How these ideas that inhabit us are social and shared, we can easily see that we do not have two hundred options of making sense of life, as vulgar liberalism tells us, but only these two streams we are describing. From them flows everything we can see and feel as being worthy of value. Although we are blind to this practical efficacy of the moral hierarchies in our lives, as we can only see the most obvious action of money and of power, it can be shown in its effects and consequences in each one of us, providing we reflect a little.

Both Bourdieu, a Frenchman, and Taylor, a Canadian, however, suppose that the "dignity of the useful producer" were something generalized in modern society. After all, both in France and Canada the vast majority of the population is "worthy", i.e. has access to the social conditions of dignity in the sense formulated here. Although Bourdieu (1963) has analyzed the marginalized of Algeria, he and every other European or American thinker tends to perceive of the phenomenon of marginality as a transient trait, in the case of the transition from dispossessed farmworker to the city, as this particular transition actually belongs to the past in Europe and the US.

The existence of entire social classes below the "dignity" line is, however, a permanent phenomenon. In Brazil and in large parts of the world there is a social class, which is also the largest on the planet, that is notable for its absence of the very conditions to carry out useful activity in the present context of the knowledge society (Souza et al. 2009). This "untouchable" class includes more than 30 percent of the population in contemporary Brazil and much more in Africa and South Asia. This unknown class exists in all capitalist societies but its size is larger and its living conditions are worse in the global South.

Taylor and Bourdieu have not sufficiently acknowledged existence below the line of dignity. But they have not even seen the dividing line at the top of society, which we call the line of aloofness. This comes as no surprise, as the aloof are hardly accessible, precisely because they are aloof. None of us ever meets a member of old and rich families, the heir of a large business conglomerate or the high nobility. There is basically no research about this class and they do not even appear in the media.

This class is aloof of everyday life and aloof of classification and judgment. Its members are also aloof of labor. They do not have to work, neither to prove their dignity nor to make money. Achievement, merit, recognition and fame are no values that they would need to pursue. They do not have to be disciplined, normal or justified. The only thing you may ever need as a member of this class is your business card but even this is unlikely, as you will hardly ever meet a person who does not know who you are. This class runs boards and charities but not political parties and everyday business affairs.

The dominant class has always "achieved" what the middle classes are striving for. They finance the elite educational institutions, charity foundations, important cultural events and political parties. While the upper middle and middle classes consist of lawyers, doctors, and top managers, the dominant class owns the organizations that employ them. The dominant class does not have to "prove" itself to be worthy of its privileges, it does not have to struggle for money, power and recognition. Everything is already there from birth.

In our interviews all around the world, very few people considered themselves lazy – most of them members of the aloof class. Labor is for the lower classes. But the dominant position is still legitimized on the basis of achievement. Expressions referring to oneself are "willing to achieve", "committed", "leadership qualities", "outstanding capabilities". The members of the dominant class think of themselves as a species apart. They are not like the rest of the population, which is somewhat paltry. Their superior qualities are innate and absolute. The other classes cannot possibly attain them.

In order to understand contemporary Brazil, the dynamics toward the lower end of the class hierarchy are more important than the dominant class. In Brazil, the lowest class is sometimes called an "under-proletariat", a mere residual concept of proletariat that explains nothing. What is under-proletariat, after all? A little below proletariat? How far below? And why? What is its specificity? The principal question is not answered. In a certain sense, what should be explained is swept beneath the carpet. Worse still is the European term "precariat", which implies something like failure. Precarious for Europeans is that group, which no longer enjoys the guarantees and security of the European social democratic pact and which is now on the defensive. This has nothing to do with the Brazilian case, which has never had a social democratic pact.

While the Brazilian left speaks of a "precariat" or "under-proletariat", the conservatives apply the scheme of income classes. The lowest class becomes a mere arbitrary number, as classes E and D, intending to circumscribe a reality that cannot be understood. The differences between individuals and classes are supposed to be captured by such superficial criteria – which are more an effect than a cause of poverty. This now dominant pseudo-explanation does not explain the main point: how and why do countless individuals find themselves in this situation of such misery while others do not? It is this, in the end, that is so necessary to understand.

This question lies at the origin of our study of classification and disqualification constructed by the idea of "dignity". The starting point was Bourdieu's insight into the practical power of the invisible line of social distinction and legitimation of privilege, the idea of "sensibility" of aesthetic taste in France. In the same way that the French case can be generalized for all modern societies wrapped up in the challenge of covering up unjust privileges by subtle and imperceptible means, the idea of "dignity" in Brazil can be generalized, to a large extent, to all societies with large numbers of marginalized and excluded people.

As capitalist societies make claims of being fair and meritocratic, these are the two "invisible lines" that legitimize the separation in society between those who are noble and superior and those who are inferior and vulgar. Even if the two lines of "sensibility" and of "dignity" become mixed up and are fluid at their borders, the dividing line of "sensibility" separates, above all, the classes of privilege – the upper and middle classes – from the lower classes. It is the good taste of the privileged, supposedly innate and from birth, that justifies their superiority not in law, formally egalitarian, but in the nonreflected and unconscious solidarities and prejudices in the everyday lives of all of us.

In the way that the reproduction of the privileges of the middle class is invisible, the middle class is the class par excellence of the myth of the "meritocracy". Supposedly, their greater competence and intelligence are the root of the privileges of this class, which would be deserved and fair. Like every privileged class, the middle class also wants to legitimize and give the appearance of justice to what is granted by chance and reproduction of an unjust privilege. It is chance because one does not choose the family, or rather social class, into which one is born. It is unjust because it condemns those who are born into a given family or social class without guilt for their miserable and flagrantly unjust fate.

In the case of Brazil, the greatest single difference is the historical construction of a class of "disqualified", forgotten, abandoned and despised by the whole of society, whose main attribute is precisely the partial or complete absence of the condition and capacity that define "dignity". Obviously, this lack of dignity is produced by a perverse, foolish and unequal society. It is perverse because of the apparent culpability of the victim of abandonment, as if anyone would choose to be poor and humiliated, and foolish and unequal because the importance of a long-term inclusive strategy is not perceived to be necessary for the wealth and well-being of the whole of society.

The line of "dignity" dividing individuals and entire social classes into worthy and unworthy of respect and the capacity of performance in the labor market helps us to see both the dividing line between the working class and the socially excluded as well as the redoubled and amplified prejudice of the upper layers of society in relation to the latter. This discussion shows that the recent transformations of Brazilian society are precisely to do with the ascension of the excluded and with the reaction of the middle sectors to this ascension.

The construction of the moralist hierarchy

We have seen that capitalism, albeit with important differences, reproduces nonreflected and unarticulated hierarchies to complement, in actual practice socially, the explicit formal equality with a real implicit and disguised inequality. In this way, privileges can be reproduced which are apparently fair and egalitarian. If the unarticulated hierarchies of good taste and useful work are universal, each society can construct other invisible hierarchies from their historical past with the same objective of reproducing privileges giving the impression of justice. This probably lies at the root of the social configuration that enabled the coup against Dilma Rousseff in 2016.

We have seen that there is an "invisible line" that separates sensitive men and women of "good taste" from vulgar men and women of "bad taste" in the lower classes. We have also seen that there is another invisible line separating the "worthy" from the "unworthy". If in the former case the social distinction by the supposed "good taste" creates a symbolic legitimacy beyond formal legality whose efficacy in justifying unjust privileges is beyond any defense, the division is more severe in the case of "dignity". This second invisible line separates the "human" from the "subhuman", as we never reflect on it.

In the end, the substance of what it is to be human is not a natural given as we imagine. The level of humanity is always a variable and differential social construction. In capitalist societies, as we have seen, this minimum level is constructed from the capacity of contribution of each person to socially useful labor. But in contemporary capitalism, to be able to carry out useful labor requires certain capabilities that are ever more challenging to members of the lower classes. Useful labor literally requires the incorporation of knowledge, the embodiment of complex practices and discipline. In fact, as we have seen, receiving the necessary stimuli from the cradle for the effort of learning is the main class privilege of the middle class, which makes the indefinite reproduction of this privilege possible.

The line of "dignity", it should be highlighted once again, does not deal with substantive values we see in received wisdom, but rather with the existence of a certain heritage of dispositions or capacities that enable the learning of a function or useful labor. This differential learning will later on enable or disable the exercising of any useful function in the market or in the state. The learning process or the absence of it will therefore decide on the outcome of the social competition of everyone against everyone for all the scarce resources, whether they be material or not. This means that apart from the moneyed at the top, the classes are engaged in a battle for appropriation of cultural capital in the various levels of complexity and recognition that is the decisive factor for the social hierarchy.

This is fundamental to our argument. It is fundamental for us to understand the variable attitude of the dominant class and the conservative middle class in the coup of 2016. The principal issue is that the moneyed of Brazil can see themselves as beyond the social struggle, as they are aloof. This is also the typical attitude of a dominant class that does not identify itself with society as a whole. We criticize our slave-owning past, which has merely been "forgotten" and condemned to return in different clothes. The attitude of the dominant class is extremely myopic, with short term and exploitative logic, just like the old slave-owning class. We have inherited from slavery not only the subhumans of all colors and "races", animalized by abandonment and dealt with as subhumans in real everyday interactions. We have also inherited the cynicism and indifference. The posture of our dominant class, which reflects this indifference, is more or less as follows: "As long as I retain my dominant position, what should I care about the social arrangement that makes this possible?"

The middle class does not have that luxury. It sees itself in competition with the other social classes for the privileged access to valuable cultural capital. At the same time, this middle class has a comparatively privileged position. It can draw on the labor of the lowest classes, who help them save time and energy as domestic workers and hard laborers, so that the middle class can dedicate themselves to profitable productive activities. There is an obvious exploitation carried out by the middle class, first of the manual work of cleaners and domestic maids (to this day the occupation responsible for the highest portion of female employment in Brazil), and then the low-paid work of the countless informal and tough jobs. Just as was done with the slaves in the city streets of the nineteenth century and the domestic slaves, the Brazilian middle class is exploiting the work of people they consider subhuman.

The concrete proof of this symbolic racism is abundant. Running over a poor "subhuman" has never been a crime in Brazil. Few middle-class persons have ever been convicted of this. The indiscriminate killings of poor people by the police has always been an informal public policy in the country, with much support from the middle class. An efficient police force is desired to "clean up" the streets. Help for poor people has always been considered cheap populism by this class. The never criticized slave-owning tradition has molded the privileged classes in Brazil, conditioning the cynicism and the haughty indifference. It has also conditioned the contempt – turning into hate depending on the circumstance – of our conservative middle class for the marginalized and those abandoned to their own fate.

In the early twenty-first century, the social assistance policies of the Worker's Party (PT) governments – transfer of income, social and racial quotas and encouragement toward university studies – have perhaps been the greatest effort made toward social inclusion of the marginalized class in Brazil. No "new middle class" has been created, as claimed in the government propaganda, but this effort has helped to show that no class, not even the "unworthy", is condemned to its fate forever. Although the tradition line of the "unworthy" is constructed via precarious familial socialization – which in turn conditions the precariousness of the schooling socialization, which further conditions the future economic exclusion in the competitive labor market – improvement is always possible.

Although improvement has been driven by virtually full employment, rising mass consumption, economic growth, investments in infrastructure, recovery of productive chains such as oil and gas, as well as a wave of optimism, which the country had not seen in decades, not everyone liked what they saw. Economically there were few losers, as the profits of financial capital continued under fair winds. Perhaps the upper portion of the middle class had a few losers economically (Neri 2012). But in politics, frequently the rational arguments are not the most decisive ones.

Despite the virtuous economic cycle having boosted the economy as a whole, many, especially in the traditional middle class, did not like having to share social spaces that had once been reserved for them with the "new barbarians" of the ascending lower classes. Complaints multiplied of airports having become noisy and full as had only happened before in bus stations, adolescents of the ascending classes were perceived as invaders in shopping centers once exclusive to the real middle class in episodes known as *rolezinhos*, or flash-mob style gatherings, while the entry of millions of new drivers to the roads of the large cities led to class prejudice. There was a diffused discomfort in the traditional middle class that could not be understood with rational reasons. To a large extent, the greater the proximity between social classes, both physically and in the habits of consumption, the more it precipitated and explained a racism of class that had previously been silent and exercised only in the private world.

The results of the last elections for president of the republic (2002, 2006, 2010 and 2014) showed a division of class that had grown and been consolidated over the years, and which finally exploded into open aggression. The racism of class was revealed in various ways during the whole of the Lula period. The middle class and its dominant conservative segment were never able to swallow a president with a lower-class way of behavior and his football meta-phors. The Europeanized Fernando Henrique Cardoso is the image of the country that the traditional middle class wanted to see reflected abroad. But until June 2013, all these complaints were made privately, within the family and in circles of friends, as it is problematic in Brazil to explain irritations typical of symbolic racism that go back to our slave-owning origins.

In this context, the "moralist line" was constructed as yet another way of producing internal solidarity among the privileged and of allowing apparently legitimate forms of exercising prejudice and class racism against those below. The moralist line is the imaginary dividing line that separates those who see themselves as superior and who are scandalized by corruption in the political parties and nationalized industry, from those who are not conscious of this matter. The feeling of superiority is constructed by the supposed ownership of a moral sensibility that only educated sectors of the middle class have. Therefore, it was the lack of education and of intelligence of the lower-class sectors that led them to, for example, continue to vote for the Worker's Party even after the Mensalão scandal. The line of morality therefore allows the votes and the worldviews of some, in this case certain segments of the middle class, to be considered better and more rational than those of others, namely, the lower classes who are disqualified as irrational and ignorant populists.

In reality, the relationship can easily be inverted. The lower classes who see politics as a fight between the rich and themselves do not act so irrationally after all. Whereas sectors of the middle class who judge themselves well informed after consuming their daily dose of media venom, and who allow themselves to be manipulated by the dominant class and their interests, are not as intelligent or as rational as they believe. The problem is that the moralist line is an old construction in Brazil. It began with the scientific prestige of figures such as Sérgio Buarque (2001; first published 1936) and continues to penetrate the schools and universities with the aura of critical knowledge. It was also present in all other coups d'état, always against the political attempts to mitigate the abysmal inequality in Brazil.

With the rise to power of the Worker's Party on the basis of lower-class votes, countless stand-in newspaper and television journalists and conservative intel-lectuals kept on repeating that the votes for the party were from people without formal education or understanding of the world. A less legitimate vote, so to speak. Since the Mensalão scandal, the dividing line between the educated and informed on the one hand and those who were hardly educated and misinformed on the other was increasingly interpreted as a division between those with greater or lesser sensibility to the question of state "corruption".

As in the cases already examined, the construction of the perception of state corruption as a sign of intelligence and moral vigor allows a revitalization and legitimation of the factual inequality. As with all moral lines of separation by solidarity and implicit prejudice which are never taken on as such, it is necessary to animalize the others and label them as cognitively and morally inferior in order to enable the feeling of justified and legitimate superiority. Rational and irrational interests can be satisfied simultaneously. Like the moneyed elite, the middle class has a rational interest in the permanence of low wages for the poor. They also have a mixture of rational and irrational interests in the destruction of the fragile welfare state constructed for the strengthening of the inclusion process. There are all kinds of interests in the expansion of the physical and social distance of the lower classes. Given their unconscious background, they are not necessarily rational.

A significant portion of the middle class interpreted the uncomfortable closer physical proximity of the lower classes in social spaces of consumption once exclusive to the middle class as the first step in a process that could mean a threat to the real privileges of earnings and prestige. This view is irrational, as the quality of the incorporation of cultural capital typical of the middle class is different. The actual social position of the middle class is not threatened by this type of inclusion. But for those used to the isolation of exclusive spaces, it is understandable that the fear of sharing such spaces be transformed into fear of the dispute for real class privileges.

The unremitting manipulative media attack on the Worker's Party and the concatenated attack on Lula were not personal attacks or on specific parties. They were attacks on a successful policy of inclusion of the lower classes that Lula and the Worker's Party represented. This social inclusion which, despite all the failures one can point to, had a historical meaning that shall not be forgotten. The selective combat against corruption by the press and their allies on the state apparatus was merely the pretext to combat a redistributive policy. If corruption were the real problem, greater emphasis would be given to the institutional aspects to avoid buying politics and administration with money. What we saw, however, was a show of hypocrisy and of persecution against Lula and the Worker's Party, leaving other parties and politicians to the side. Greater falsity and hypocrisy would be impossible. That many believed in this farce is due to the rational and irrational interests from the most conservative part of the middle class that "emotionally" hungered for a pretext to express their class hatred.

It was a joining of unprecedented symbolic violence, led by the press, with a social base that was anxious to mask their class disdain, repressed during the previous years of the Worker's Party government, under a hypocritical but apparently rational guardian of decency and morality. The coup involved the conscious manipulation of the fear of a social class that saw itself as threatened.

It was this fear, represented by the rapid social ascension of the lower sectors, that helped consolidate a class barrier against the inclusive project of the Worker's Party. What was lacking was a suitable narrative, a discourse that made the irrational fear rational, and a charismatic leader with the same weight that Lula had with the lower classes. The discourse was the moralist legitimation typical of the selective combat against corruption. The charismatic leader was the judge Sérgio Moro, who "exemplified" and synthesized in his manners and in his actions, or rather in his aesthetic and in his morals, the hunger of this class for a redemptive moral cleansing of the country.

Conclusion

This chapter has studied the social classes of Brazil and their characteristics as well as the dividing lines between them. This analysis was used to explain recent political events in the country. The main argument of the chapter lies in the demonstration that persistent class lines exist in capitalist countries. Even though these lines are invisible and contradict the egalitarian foundation myths of contemporary capitalist societies, they are incorporated and exert a practical influence in much of our social and even political behavior.

Because the Brazilian class structure emerged historically out of the hierarchy of a slave-holding society, its internal configuration and composition differs greatly from that of Germany and Laos. However, all three societies are developing similar dividing lines between the classes, namely the lines of dignity, expressivity and aloofness. In Laos, these lines are not yet very pervasive, while even in Brazil and Germany they do not entirely explain the class structure, as the Brazilian middle class and the German fighter class both comprise two tradition lines and habitus groups that do not fully correspond to the order of classes.

Still, the mechanisms of the production and reproduction of inequality are similar or possibly even identical in all three countries. This is even true for a country in which a seemingly very unique precapitalist structure of inequality continues to play a prominent role. The relation of caste and class in India, the subject of our next chapter, allows us to shed more light not only on the structures of inequality around the world, but also the mechanisms producing them.

Note

1 The Brazilian research team consisted of Brand Arenari, Roberto Dutra Torres, Emerson Ferreira Rocha, Fabrício Maciel, Emanuelle Silva and Ricardo Visser.

5 The Indian story of inequality

The previous chapters have outlined the class structure of capitalist societies, the development of classes out of precapitalist hierarchies and the construction of dividing lines between the classes. This chapter brings together these three aspects of social inequality and combines them with a seemingly very particular and traditional type of inequality, which is caste. We argue that even for the emergence of the new middle class and the top professions, caste plays an important role and informs the emerging capitalist class structure.

This chapter draws a bit less on our empirical material than the preceding chapters, for two reasons. First, it includes even more historical information than the chapter on Laos. Second, our research on India has not reached the same level of comprehensiveness as the research on the other three countries. After all, India has four times as many inhabitants as the other three countries combined. However, it would not have been possible to write this chapter without our previous research on caste and our interviews.[1]

The chapter first briefly reviews the discussions about the notion of caste. It then gives an equally brief overview of recent developments in India. The remainder of the chapter deals with the intersection of caste and class. One section outlines caste today and another one class in the contemporary scenario. The main part of the chapter then focuses on their intersection in the Indian middle class. This discussion links up with the debates about the middle classes in Brazil as well as with the emergence of a new middle class and a laboring class in Laos.

Orientalism and caste

In the classical Western imaginations, particularly those influenced by the Orientalist and colonial modes of thinking, India has almost always been viewed as a society founded on the value of inequality and hierarchy. Though hierarchy is believed to be a feature of every traditional society, it was only in India that it supposedly acquired an all-pervasive nature, institutionalized and entrenched through its religious tradition and ideology. The obvious reference point here is to the practice of caste and its presumed centrality to the Indian way of life, its economy, its culture and its everyday social relations.

When the French sociologist Louis Dumont (1971) chose to title his book on India as *Homo Hierarchicus*, he was not only trying to describe the core features of the caste system or the foundational values of the Indian/Hindu social order, but he was also proposing to construct the social order in India as the contrasting "other" of the modern West, the *homo equalis*. In his theory, everything about India was different from the Western way of life and its foundational codes. While the modern West was founded on the idea of equality, hierarchy, a rigid and naturalized form of inequality, marked social life in India. Even when differences or inequalities of class and power continued to be present in the modern West, they were viewed as being epiphenomenal in nature and not constitutive, as was assumed to be in the case of India. For example, the differences of status that persist in the Western cultures were presumably produced by the differences of economic wealth and political power born out of the free market and a reward system based on equal opportunity. In contrast, status or caste in Indian society was supreme and emanated out of its collective tradition, which encompassed structures of power and economic systems.

Writing in 1962, Myron Weiner, an American political scientist, also found India subscribing to a culture of inequality as no other tradition did:

> [P]erhaps no other major society in recent history has known inequalities so gross or so long preserved. In the traditional civilizations of Islam and China, the ideal if not always the practice of equality had an honorable and often commanding place in the culture. But in India the notion that men should remain in the same occupation and station of life as their forefathers was enshrined in religious precepts and social custom.[2]

Over the past decades, such Orientalist essentializations of India's past have been very widely criticized by a range of scholars. Such notions tended to simplify the complexities and diversities of the realities on the ground. Not only did the nature and form of caste-based differences vary across regions of the subcontinent, quite like any other social formation, structures of hierarchy have also been contested from within through a range of individual and collective human actions, such as the so-called devotional theistic movements. Some of these movements presented elaborate critiques of the Brahmanical system of hierarchy and offered alternative modes of transcendence and social organization underlying the values of humanism, equality and universalism (see Omvedt 2008). They also produced new communities of believers who organized their faith practices and religious institutions around the values of equality and human dignity.[3]

Furthermore, caste never existed as a unitary system of hierarchy as it is popularly presented in the textbooks of social anthropology or sociology. Its practice and arrangements or systems of hierarchy differed across regions, depending on regional differences of ecology, economy and local histories. It also evolved and changed with time in response to changing political regimes and their ideological thrusts. Caste was never as encompassing a reality as it is made out to be in the textbooks of social anthropology. Social structures of agrarian formations did not always correspond to the textual notion of *varna* hierarchy. Materialities of everyday economic life actively interacted and intersected with caste. In turn, caste shaped and influenced economic differences and political regimes (Dirks 2001; Guha 2013; Jodhka 2015).

However, this is not to deny the significance of caste as a critical system of domination, an axis of inequality in India, in the past or in the present. The assertion being made here is simply the fact that such an idea or notion of caste does not describe and explain everything about inequalities in India. It never did. Caste is not simply a religious tradition of the Hindus, frozen in time until its exposure to colonial modernity; once exposed, it was supposed to gradually decline and eventually disappear with the process of economic growth, urbanization and expansion of modern values. Such a perspective also suggests that the capitalist transformation will, on its own, produce a secular mode of social organization, a radical shift to the capitalist mode of production where inequalities are based only on economic criteria achieved through individual merit. Thus, the category that describes such differences ought to be class.

It is not only the functionalist framework of modernization theory that conceptualizes the process of social change in countries of the global South through such binaries (from caste to class or tradition to modernity). Even the Marxist scholarship on countries like India tends to look at history from a teleological framing through the category of mode of production, where the ascendance of capitalist mode of production is presumed to inevitably destroy precapitalist relational structures like the caste. One of the earliest applications of this thesis in the Indian context could be found in the writings of A. R. Desai (1948) and later in the framing of "mode of production debate" in Indian agriculture during the 1970s by some of the leading Marxist economists (see Thorner 1982). Taking a cue from the writings of Karl Marx on the impact of British rule on India, Desai famously argued that the introduction and spread of capitalist mode of production during the colonial rule began to weaken, presumably for the first time, the idea and structure of caste and gave birth to a fundamentally new economy structured around class. Such a teleological view of social life and history tends to blind us to the ground realities and complex ways in which inequalities persist and are reproduced.

The broader context

After its independence from colonial rule in 1947, the Indian state tried to follow the Soviet model of economic growth, albeit partially. The new elites who succeeded the colonial masters were greatly inspired by the idea of state-led planned economic development that would produce quick results and lessen the pain of developing a poor country into a capitalist market regime. This was perhaps also a historic necessity if the country had to gain a measure of autonomy from global capital, given that the native capital had no capacity to invest in building infrastructure and basic industry, crucially required for economic growth of a country where the majority lived in hunger and deprivation. During the early decades of the twentieth century, the region had witnessed a series of famines when thousands perished for sheer unavailability of food. Though the colonial rulers had introduced a Western-style formal educational system, the large majority of Indians were educationally deprived and knew no letters.

Over the seven decades after 1947, India's economy and its influence in the world have grown quite significantly. With nearly 1.25 billion people, India has the second largest population in the world today and is fast catching up with China. India has a much younger population. Since the early 1990s, India, along with China, has also been among the most rapidly growing economies of the world, at around 7 percent annually. Much of this growth has been urban-oriented, and mostly occurred in the service sector. Even though the industrial economy has also been growing, its share in the national income is only in the range of 25 to 30 percent. In contrast, the service sector contributes to a little more than half of the entire national income. India has also seen a significant decline in the economic value of its agricultural sector, even when it continues to formally engage nearly half of its working population. By the second decade of the twenty-first century, the share of agriculture in the national income came down to less than one third of what it was in the early 1950s, which works out to be only around one seventh of the total national income (around 13 percent).

However, change in India's demographic structure has been much slower. Even in 2011, when the last census was carried out, a little more than two-thirds of Indians lived in its more than half a million rural settlements. The pace of urbanization has been rather slow with only around 31 percent of Indians living in urban areas. However, given the number of its total population, the absolute size of the "urban" in India is very large with some of the most populated cities in the world being part of the country. More importantly, with change in its economic structure, the country has witnessed a significant shift in balance of power, away from the rural rich and toward the corporate elite and urban-based middle classes.

India has often been described as a land of contradictions. While the country continues to have the largest number of chronically poor, more than Sub-Saharan Africa, it is also among the top five countries in terms of the number of dollar billionaires in the world today. India is among the emerging economies of the world and already figures among the top ten wealthiest countries. If it continues to grow at the current pace, it may soon be among the top five countries. The absolute number of rich Indians in terms of purchasing power parity – middle and upper-middle classes – would be more than the total population of most countries of Western Europe.

As we have been arguing in this book, inequalities of income and wealth ownership tell us little about the structures of domination, which produce relations and experiences of inequality. These structures of domination exist everywhere and they are often comparable, but they also need to be understood in their local contexts in terms of their histories and the patterns of their intersections. The so-called traditional structures, such as the Indian caste system, do not disappear with development of a capitalist economy or urbanization unless they are actively targeted. In the absence of targeted action, they tend to survive and alter their forms and formats. In the remaining pages of this chapter, we discuss the specifics of the Indian context.

Caste, past and present

As indicated in the previous section, the popular textbook view of caste presents it as a unique feature of Indian culture. In this understanding, caste is also presented as an ancient institution based on the ideas of *varna, karma* and *dharma* presented most explicitly in a classic Hindu text called the *Manusmriti*. These ideas translated into a hierarchical society structured around the notions of purity and pollution. The *varna* system divided the Hindus into four or five mutually exclusive and hierarchically ranked categories with the Brahmins at the top, followed by the Kshatriyas, the Vaishyas and the Shudras. Beyond the four *varnas* were the *achhoots* (the untouchables), sometimes classified as a fifth category. Even though the hierarchy was inscribed in ritual terms, it also structured almost every aspect of social and economic life and survived without much change for centuries.

While this popular view of caste still figures in many textbooks of sociology and social anthropology introducing Indian society, it has also been very widely criticized, conceptually as well as empirically, and has been abandoned by most serious students of Indian society. Scholars working on India have convincingly shown that it was primarily Western writers, the Orientalists and colonial administrators, who constructed such a view in the nineteenth century. As these scholars argue, colonial ideologues wanted to portray the region as having been eternally stuck in its cultural past and incapable of progressing on the path of history by itself (Cohn 1996; Dirks 2001; Guha 2013). Such a view thus provided a built-in justification for the colonial subjugation of India.

The empirical scholarship on the subject also questions the simplified religion-centric view of caste. Sociologists, social anthropologists and historians have extensively documented the fluid nature of hierarchies and the diverse modes of its formations. While hierarchies existed on the ground, their structures and operations varied significantly across different regions of the subcontinent. Caste had also not been a static and closed cultural reality that reproduced itself only through religious ritual and traditional beliefs. As mentioned earlier, being a part of social life, caste differences were structured and shaped also by economic processes, ecological possibilities and the nature of political regimes of a given region (see Srinivas 1955, 1962; Beteille 1974; Charsley and Karanth 1998; Gupta 2000; Jodhka 2012, 2015).

As we have been arguing in this chapter, the popular Orientalist view of caste also shared its notion of social change with functionalist theories on the subject that predicted its demise through the process of modernization (see Chapter 1). The colonial rulers had presumably unleashed such a process by introducing Western-style secular education, industrial technology and modern frames of governance. Interestingly, many among the early Indian nationalists also took rather easily to this evolutionist view of caste and its possible modern futures. Independence from colonial rule, many of them believed, would accelerate the process of modernization of social life through economic growth and democratic politics, guided by a liberal-progressive constitution and gradually end caste. Against this background we have to ask: What has been happening to caste over the past century or so? How has it changed or declined? If it persists, what makes it reproduce itself? How could the category of caste make sense of emerging patterns of inequalities in contemporary India?

India's independence from colonial rule did accelerate the process of social and economic change, and these changes have also had a significant impact on the social order of caste. A variety of efforts and processes from "below", from "above" and from the "side" have brought these changes about. Persistent and active mobilizations by those located lower down in the hierarchical order have gone a long way in delegitimizing the ideology and cultural value of the traditions associated with caste. The values and aspirations for dignified life as citizens of a democratic country have successfully eroded the earlier notions of *karma*, the inevitability of destiny attached to one's past birth, almost everywhere in the subcontinent. Since the early 1980s, such mobilizations from the margins of Indian society have only grown, and some scholars have gone to the extent of describing them as a source of a "silent revolution" (Jaffrelot 2003). Notwithstanding diversities and divergences, growing politicization of the "backwards" and increasing assertions by the Dalits, the ex-untouchables have fundamentally altered the grammar of Indian social and political life (Pai 2002).

After independence, the democratic Indian state institutionalized a system of quotas or reservations for the most deprived communities and listed them as Scheduled Castes (SCs). Similarly, some other social groups who were seen to be deprived because of their relative isolation from mainland India were classified as Scheduled Tribes (STs). Under this system, seats approximate to their proportions in the Indian population were kept reserved for them in state-funded educational institutions, government jobs and legislative bodies up to the highest level, the Indian Parliament. The constitutional provisions in the form of a reservation policy have not only enabled a process of social and economic mobility among the ex-untouchable castes but have also been instrumental in producing a modern leadership from within these communities.

India's quota system has expanded over the years. In addition to the quotas mandated by the national government, some provincial governments have had their own quota regimes. Following recommendations of various commissions set up by the government of India to identify communities other than those listed as Scheduled Castes, who remain "backward", the union government also decided to reserve jobs and seats in state-funded educational institutions for the Other Backward Classes (OBCs). Even though the Indian courts have fixed a ceiling of 50 percent seats for quotas, the demand for quotas has continued to grow. Such state policies and other initiatives from "above" have also changed caste.

Furthermore, the larger processes and the nature of social, economic and political transformations taking place in the country have also altered caste relations in a variety of ways. For example, the agrarian transformations ushered in by the success of the Green Revolution in some parts of the country, and the development of industry in urban centers, have made many of the traditional caste occupations redundant. At the same time, they have also provided new opportunities for employment outside the older economic order. State investments in rural development and agricultural growth have provided a positive impetus to this process. The Indian agriculture gradually moved toward formalized and capitalist frames of production and social organization. Traditional hierarchies and old structures of dependency, including the traditional hierarchies of caste, gradually declined (Mendelsohn 1993; Charsley and Karanth 1998; Jodhka 2002; Srinivas 2003; Kapur et al. 2010).

Class

Unlike caste, the concept of class has been used by social scientists and policy actors and administrators generally as an objective category for aggregation and classification. Class status is generally assigned to a person or a household (not a group or a collectivity) on the basis of one's income/wealth, the "market situation" or one's position in the mode of production. However, despite generic notions of class or its use for describing economic inequalities in the modern capitalist society, class has also had an emic dimension and is deployed as a popular category of self-description and identification even in societies like India.

For example, writing on the social structure and inequalities in the agrarian economy of India, Daniel Thorner (1956) used a popular native classification to identify and classify rural households in class categories. He argued that on the basis of (a) the form of income from the soil, (b) the type of rights on the soil, and (c) the form of labor or work performed on the land, agrarian population of India could be divided broadly into three class categories: the *maliks*, proprietors or landlords who rarely work on land but had control over large tracks of land; the *kisans*, the self-cultivating peasants with smaller holdings; and the *mazdoors* who are mostly landless and earn their living by working for the proprietor landlords as tenants or wage-laborers. This is not simply a classification imposed by an outsider economist or a census enumerator. They are also used as relational categories and as categories of self-identification in different regions of India. Though the terms or words used may differ, this broad three-fold classification has been a cultural mode of describing differences and hierarchies of agrarian life in rural India (see Beteille 1974).

Another important milestone in the Indian social science writings on inequality with class as core category was the famous debate on the dominant mode of production in Indian agriculture. Inspired by another piece of writing by Thorner (1969), economists (with a few social anthropologists also participating) carried out a rather long debate on the nature of agrarian change in India, following the introduction of Green Revolution technology during the late 1960. Using

Marxist method and its categories, they debated the nature of emerging and dominant modes of production in Indian agriculture. Some of them also identified the nature of social classes in Indian agriculture and patterns of their relationships. They mostly worked with the Leninist model of agrarian classes with landlords and rich farmers in the dominant role and tenants/sharecroppers and landless laborers in subordinated position. In between were the middle peasants, who mostly worked with their family labor and cultivated their own plots of land. Given their positions in the structure of agrarian relations, neither did they exploit anyone, nor did others exploit them. Some of the economists also reported a process of differentiation and proletarianization taking place with the steady spread of the capitalist mode of production in the agrarian economy.[4]

This debate on determining the nature of agrarian change and characterizing the emerging mode of production was over by the early 1980s. However, a large majority of Indian economists, who are also the development actors, continue to use the category of class for economic classification of the rural populations, largely based on landownership status and the acreage ownership structure, to discuss the nature of inequalities and other dynamics of change in India's agrarian economy.

A little while later, in an interesting and influential book, another Indian economist, Pranab Bardhan (1984), identified a set of classes in his analysis of India's political economy and its structure of domination. He identified three "dominant propertied classes" that ruled the economic life of independent India. These were the industrial capitalist class, the rich farmers and the professionals, who included civic and military bureaucracy. He also argued that among the three dominant classes, the professional class was the most dynamic with much greater possibility of upward mobility via education.

It is this class of professionals that makes for India's vibrant middle class, which has been a subject of much discussion since the early 1990s. As discussed earlier, the Indian middle class has also been a site of much contestation around the subjects of caste and mobility. Perhaps much more than in the discussion of the poor or the rich, the concept of 'class' in India has been deployed in writings on the middle class. During the British colonial period, in the early decades of the nineteenth century, the term "middle class" began to be used for a newly emergent group of people in urban centers, mostly in Calcutta, Bombay and Madras, three cities founded by the colonial masters. Over time, this middle class spread its presence to other urban centers of the subcontinent as well. After independence from colonial rule, the size of the Indian middle class grew manifold. This time again, it was largely through state action and expansion. The developmental state expanded its bureaucratic reach and invested massively in public sector enterprises and laid the infrastructure for social progress and economic growth. It opened many more schools, universities, hospitals and a range of other institutions required for building a modern nation-state.

Beginning with the 1990s, the story of the Indian middle class witnessed a major shift. The pace and patterns of its growth changed with the introduction of economic reforms. The new policies of liberalization encouraged private capital to expand its spheres of investment. India's growing integration into the global economy and its cultural flows also enabled many more Indians to benefit through the opening of newer avenues of employment and mobility. As discussed earlier, by incentivizing private capital and encouraging foreign capital to invest in India, the "neoliberal" economic reforms helped the country accelerate the pace of its economic growth.

At another level, this acceleration of economic growth and expansion of the Indian middle classes, both in numbers as well as in influence, has quite fundamentally transformed the structure of Indian society and its economy, from one characterized by "a sharp contrast between a small elite and a large impoverished mass, to being one with substantial intermediate classes" (Sridharan 2008: 1). However, much of the popular discourse on the Indian middle class is focused around numbers and income categories.[5] Mostly framed in economic terms, this discourse tends to focus on the parts of Indian population that could be described as middle class almost exclusively in terms of their earnings and expenditure levels, current and prospective. By implication, it tends to focus primarily on their consumption potential in the emerging markets.

While incomes and consumption cultures are indeed important aspects of social and economic life, "middle class" is not simply an economic category but also a relational structure. The growth and expansion of the middle class also indicates a move toward the emergence of a new kind of society. As sociologists Landry and Marsh (2011) rightly argue, "the emergence of a middle class marks a decisive moment in a nation's history. It indicates an open rather than a closed opportunity structure, a society with the chance of upward mobility and achievement beyond subsistence" (374).

The obvious point of reference in this framework in the Indian case would be the caste. The system of caste-based hierarchies molded social and ritual life of the common people. It also shaped occupations, opportunities and rewards. Caste produced an environment of exclusions, segregations and avoidance, a culture marked by rigid status hierarchies and imperious structures of authority. Thus, the questions that become relevant in this context are: How does the emergence of a modern middle class negotiate with the preexisting realities of caste and cultures of rigid hierarchies, or in other words, has the rise of a middle class been accompanied by a social transformation as envisaged in the popular sociological theories of change and as promised by the Indian Constitution? What has been the nature of mobility into middle-class social locations across various caste groups and categories? How have the local cultures of hierarchy and difference influenced the emergent category of "middle class" in contemporary India?

The Indian middle class

As discussed earlier, the historical context to the birth of Indian middle class was the need of the British colonial rulers for a class of lower-level native bureaucracy that would assist them in their rule over the vast regions of the subcontinent that they had come to occupy by the early nineteenth century. They were to be "a class of persons Indian in blood and color, but English in tastes, in opinions, in morals and in intellect".[6]

As the popular narrative goes, thanks to these policies, such a class did emerge, which mediated between the colonial masters and the local masses. These middle-class individuals also became the vehicles for the spread of "superior" Western culture and its message of modernity, including the ideas of democracy. In due course, these ideas also became a source of conflict between the newly emerged middle-class Indians and the colonial rulers, eventually unfolding into the movement for independence. According to this common sense, the Western-educated middle class of India continues to be a modernizing social category and an important agent of positive social change in the Indian society, where the hold of tradition continues to be a critical source of its backwardness.

While the colonial context of its origin is indeed a fact, this celebratory representation of the Indian middle class is a myth that, to a large extent, is produced by members of the Indian middle classes themselves. It helps them perpetuate their position of privilege and power. The actual history of the Indian middle class is far more complex and different.

The Indian middle class did not just emerge as a modernizing agent out of its traditional moorings. On the contrary, there were many instances where it championed "tradition". Instead of being individualized and modern, its members actively represented and constructed local-level "sectarian" identities. The British did not always wish to change the preexisting social realities. They often absorbed them into their policy frames and reinforced or strengthened the preexisting structures of social relations. In other words, they simultaneously transformed and reinforced the preexisting structures of power relations. The Indian middle class actively participated in all these processes (see Jodhka and Prakash 2016).

The social base of recruitment of this class was also quite narrow. The British initiated a process of educating the "natives" by opening schools and colleges in different parts of the subcontinent. These educational institutions first appeared in the new colonial cities of Calcutta, Bombay and Madras. Local communities, particularly those with resources and high social standing, responded enthusiastically and sent their children for "modern" education. Unlike their Western counterparts, the social origins of this class did not lie in industry and trade, which remained under control of the British companies or local trading communities, such as the Marwaris, Khatris and Banias. While most of the educated modern professionals came from relatively privileged social backgrounds and had some connections with land, they generally occupied intermediary positions in the prevailing tenurial structure. In terms of their position in the traditional ritual hierarchies, they almost all came from relatively upper segments of the traditional caste system.

Some rich Indian families even sent their children abroad, mostly to England, for higher education in leading British universities, such as Oxford, Cambridge and London, with many returning home after securing degrees. These new native elite also brought with them modern ideas of "liberalism" and "democracy" that had become popular in Northatlantic societies after the French Revolution. Thus, they became carriers of not only British cultural values but also of modern ideas of freedom, equality and democracy. Those educated in local colleges were mostly absorbed in the colonial administrative structure. These jobs in the colonial government carried a "high" social status and became a route to acquiring middle-class positions. Over the years, a new class emerged in India. Apart from those employed in the administrative jobs of the British government, it included independent professionals, such as lawyers, medics and teachers. The size of this "educated middle class" thus continued to grow during the second half of the nineteenth century.

In some regions of the subcontinent, these newly educated individuals initiated a variety of social reform movements during the nineteenth and early twentieth centuries. The middle-class leaders of these movements worked for negotiated adaptations of Western modernity. They underlined the need for retaining what they saw as the core of the traditional religious belief and culture while simultaneously learning from Christian cultures. The narrative was to selectively reinvent past tradition and glorify it in order to claim its superiority over Western Christianity. This reinvention and glorification of India's ancient past also implied acceptance and advocacy of "tradition", albeit in a reformed format, which included the hierarchical social order of *varna* and caste, presided over by the Brahmin. Unlike in the West, where the middle classes were part of the processes of secularization and individualization, members of the Indian middle classes invested in their community identities and many worked actively toward reinvention of their perceived traditions through "reform" movements. Their quest for the so-called social reforms eventually produced "new", and sometimes more rigid, cultural boundaries across and within the preexisting communities (see Jodhka and Prakash 2016: 48–54).

As the middle class expanded in size, its political aspirations also grew. It aspired to a greater share in the state power. It is in this context that the middle class began to articulate the idea of India as an independent nation-state. However, its members recognized the need of a cultural project, of producing a larger "ethnic" and cultural community, beyond the simple agenda of social and religious reform of local level religious communities. Partha Chatterjee (1993) describes this as "classicization of tradition", which could become the foundational category of Indian nationalism. The Indian middle class thus campaigned and mobilized for a politics of citizenship by actively pursuing a sectarian agenda, even when it invoked ideas of democracy and modernity.

Independence from colonial rule in 1947 was an important turning point for the Indian middle-class story. The new elite that inherited power from the colonial rulers largely represented the upper layers of Indian society, both in terms of caste as well as class. However, they were also confronted with the task of working with diversities and differences of Indian society, poverty and disparities, the challenge of violence and communal harmony. The fault lines were many and difficult to deal with. The framing of the Indian Constitution with B. R. Ambedkar, an untouchable by caste, as the chair of its drafting committee had an important symbolic value for the new nation as it tried to signal that independent, democratic India was to transcend caste. Membership of the Constituent Assembly also represented other forms of social diversities. Besides laying down a framework for a democratic governance system, the Indian Constitution also recognized caste as a continued source of disparities and deprivations and put in place a set of measures that would work toward leveling the playing field.

Even though India chose to follow the path of Western-style liberal democracy, it did so with a difference. Jawaharlal Nehru, the first prime minister of India, had also been inspired by the achievements of the then socialist-bloc countries. He initiated planning for development. Democracy and development were to help India move on the path of modernization, with the Indian state playing an active role in creating an enabling environment for economic growth with social justice. It even initiated direct participation in setting up modern industry. Besides investing directly in public sector industrial units, the state also spent a lot of resources on laying down institutional and material infrastructure required to extend its physical reach to diverse communities and regions of the subcontinent. To pursue these activities, the state required skilled human resources. The state sector thus emerged the biggest employer and the most important site for middle-class expansion. The number of those employed in the state sector went up from 5.23 million in 1956 to 15.48 million in 1980. Even though employment in the private sector also expanded, it grew at a slower rate, from 5.05 million in 1960 to 7.24 million in 1980 (Jodhka and Prakash 2016: 76).

As indicated previously, the introduction of economic reforms in the 1990s rather significantly changed the pace and pattern of economic growth in India with a clear shift toward the private sector. This is also reflected in the nature and patterns of employment. Though available data of organized sector employment reflects that the state sector still has more people on its rolls than the private sector, the trend had clearly changed. During 2010–11, the total employment in state-supported sectors was 17.55 million, lower than what it was twenty years before, in 1990–91 (19.14 million). In contrast, the organized private sector, though employing lower numbers still (11.45 million) in 2010–11, had grown significantly over the preceding twenty years (7.68 million in 1990–91).

Caste and middle-class mobility

How do these dynamics of numbers and economic changes intersect with social processes? As is evident from the preceding discussion, the available historical research suggests that the rise of the middle class in India during the British colonial period did not dent caste hierarchies. On the contrary, the middle class grew within the preexisting ascriptive frames of communities and identities.

Over the past century and more, social and economic structures, including those of caste, have seen many changes. However, while change in relational and ideological spheres is apparent, the reality of caste does not seem to be going away. Inequalities across caste groups have persisted, and in some cases they have sharpened. Caste continues to matter beyond its conventional sphere of influence, the village, its ritual life and its agrarian economy. Even after moving out of the rural areas, into an urban job or a business, individuals often remain tied to their caste. Those from the upper stratum of the caste hierarchy find caste to be a useful resource in the urban context and often feel comfortable in the company of fellow caste men and women. Almost all of them marry within their caste kinship. They form caste associations and set up caste community–based business cartels. Even when the growing anonymity of urban economy makes it difficult to sustain such monopolies, kinship networks continue to play a critical role in the reproduction of urban business (Iyer et al. 2013).

The modern corporate sector is also not free from caste. Even when they manifestly claim to be caste-blind, corporates care for the social and family backgrounds of their staff. They often screen out candidates from communities such as the Scheduled Castes, the Muslims and those from "rustic" rural backgrounds (Jodhka and Newman 2007). A recent study based on a sample of 1,000 companies reported that as many as 92.6 percent of the board members of the Indian Corporate houses are from the upper castes (44.6 percent Brahmins and 46.0 percent from various *Vaishya* castes). In contrast, the SCs and STs together made for only 3.5 percent. Even the proportion of the officially recognized communities with the baggage of backwardness, the Other Backward Classes (OBCs) who make up nearly half of India's total population, was quite negligible (3.8 percent) (Ajit et al. 2012).[7] At the upper end of the corporate management, "caste diversity is non-existent". The limited volume of empirical literature we have on social mobility in India reinforces the point that caste indeed works to block those located at the lower end of the caste hierarchy (Kumar et al. 2002; Thorat and Newman 2010; Vaid and Heath 2010).

The urban upper castes that are otherwise located in capitalist spaces work hard to preserve the privileges that come with caste, constructing boundaries around the middle class locations. In a recently published book based on prolonged fieldwork among the Brahmins of Tamil Nadu, exploring the changes brought about by their social mobility and migrations from rural settlements to urban centers over the past century and more, Fuller and Narasimhan (2015) found that although the Brahmins had all begun to see themselves as members of the middle class, they remained strongly tied to their caste identity. This identification of being Brahmin was so central to their identity as middle-class persons that the two authors chose to describe the Brahmin case of mobility as *The Making of a Middle-Class Caste* (the subtitle of their book). They write:

> [A]ll Tamil Brahmins today regard themselves as urbanites and members of the middle class, so that their caste and class status are intertwined and Tamil Brahminhood is congruent with middle classness.
>
> (Fuller and Narasimhan 2015: 210)

Another study of upper-caste Brahmins in Bangalore found them forming their associations with the clear purpose of countering the politics of democratization being articulated by the "backwards". They advocate the need of preserving traditional values, which by implication also implied protecting Brahmin caste privileges (Bairy 2009).

However, this is not to suggest that the caste system did not change at all. Despite these persisting inequalities and cultures of exclusion, India's middle-class story and its interface with caste are far more complex than a simple case of reproducing caste in a new *avatar*, this time called the middle class. Over the years, the middle-class space in India has become socially far more diverse. Even when the traditional upper castes continue to dominate, they are not the only ones who claim middle-class identity or occupy such positions in the secular and professional economies of India. Nearly seven decades of affirmative action policies for the Scheduled Castes have been able to open up possibilities of mobility even for the most deprived, the ex-untouchables. However, the quality and extent of change has been limited.

It was during the British colonial period that caste began to be enumerated. In the later years of colonial rule, the idea of affirmative action started to be framed through classification of caste communities into categories like the "depressed classes". This classification became a source of identifying communities to be listed as Scheduled Castes for the reservations policy. Furthermore, the Western-style secular education introduced by the British rulers was in principle open to all, including those from the "untouchable" communities. The colonial government also employed individuals from these communities in their administrative system. Thanks to all these policies, a few members of the "untouchable" communities and those from the other "backward" classes could study and move to urban middle-class spaces, which had so far been the monopoly of the Brahmins and other upper castes. Some of these individuals, such as Jyotiba Phule and B. R. Ambedkar in Maharashtra or E. V. Ramasamy in the south of India, initiated a range of anti-Brahmin and anti-caste movements (Omvedt 1976; Pandian 1997). They were to become a source of inspiration for the later middle classes that emerged from these communities in the post-independence period.

Perhaps the most visible effect of the quotas, particularly in the case of the Scheduled Castes, has been the emergence of a Dalit middle class. Even when their communities remain largely poor and marginalized, individuals from these communities have been able to move up to senior positions in political institutions, the bureaucracy and academia. Their experience of being middle class has been one of the struggles and challenges.

Normally, in such processes of individual mobility, the upwardly mobile individual tends to move out of his or her group of origin to another group compatible with his or her class situation. This, however, has generally not been the experience of mobile Dalits. Available empirical literature tends to show that even when such individuals move to secular employment and middle-class occupations, their identification with the communities of their origin tends to remain strong.

Why does this happen? First and foremost, economic mobility does not always lead to disappearance of prejudice against the upwardly mobile Dalits from the dominant groups who often resent the quota system and tend to see the Dalits occupying middle-class jobs as illegitimate, as if those jobs have been taken away from them in a violation of their privileged monopoly. This is exactly the same phenomenon that lies at the root of middle-class discontent with the Brazilian governments of Lula and Dilma (see Chapter 4).

In such environments of hostility, the social mobility that should accompany the individual's economic mobility becomes rather limited. Even when a Dalit occupies a high position of authority, upper-caste colleagues tend to identify him or her at first with the caste of his or her origin and only later with his or her position of authority. Such a lack of collegial acceptance produces disorientation and often anger and agitation (Jodhka 2015) among the upwardly mobile Dalits. Their responses to such situations vary. Some try to conceal their caste identity (Mallick 1997), but some others turn back to their communities with the realization that without a larger social change that gives dignity to the communities of their identity, their individual achievements remain of limited value. They become community activists. Thus, in either case, mobility to a middle-class status in such cases does not produce individualization and secularization of status (see Jodhka 2010; Prakash 2015).

Upwardly mobile SCs also find it difficult to realize their middle-class status because of the larger economic context. They are invariably the first members of their families to earn a middle-class salary. In many cases, their privileged position within the family also puts pressure on them monetarily. They are morally expected to look after their poor kin by sending home a portion of their income (Naudet 2014: 244). Even though mobility through education, followed by a job, is an individual achievement, the community tends to see educated members of their community as a "collectively shared" resource (Ciotti 2012). The imperative of "paying back" to the community often has a strong moral appeal with such successful individuals, given that an SC individual more often than not acquires education and a secure job using quotas, which are viewed as an outcome of their collective struggle for rights (Naudet 2014: 245; Jodhka 2015: 169–209).

However, notwithstanding this sense of identification with the larger caste identity and caste question, the upward mobility of SCs also inhibits their return. While they realize the need for change through political mobilizations and activism, they are no longer similar to those they have left behind and also feel a sense of alienation from their communities (Guru 2001). They tend to form their own caste-based enclaves where they feel comfortable by expanding the boundaries of their caste communities through categories such as "Dalits". This also gives them a sense of a new identity and a sense of being modern and dignified, but their social life tends to be limited to fellow Dalits (Ram 1988). Their perception of state and economy is often shaped by the prism of caste and the associated hierarchies and discriminations experienced by members of their community, if not they themselves. Hence their image and understanding of India's modernity is generally at variance with that of the dominant section of the middle class. They still look up to the state, which alone, for many of them, could be above the caste-divided institutions of civil society and market economy. Recognition of the deficits of social and cultural capital in their communities also makes them suspect advocates of free market and meritocratic regimes. Even when SCs mobilize for their own increased participation in the neoliberal market economy, they seek quotas and state support.

Class and/as caste

The site of "middle class" in today's India provides an interesting window into the nature of emerging inequalities. It also enables us to integrate the transformations being unleashed by the dynamics of rural-to-urban migrations and aspirations for mobility in the lower rungs of society. A good example of this is what has come to be described as the aspirational middle class. The idea of the aspirational middle class has even become an important category of political discourse in neoliberal India. The election manifesto of a major national party describes them as those "who have risen from the category of poor and are yet to stabilize in the middle class", the "neo middle class".[8]

These "upwardly mobile poor" are invariably young men and women who have acquired modern education through one of the hundreds of thousands of colleges spread across the country giving degree/diploma courses in information and technology, marketing, law, finance, business or tourism. Many of them are from traditionally "dominant" and relatively upper castes in the rural areas. Educated and in pursuit of their aspirations, they move from rural areas to urban locations by selling parental assets. They often enter into relatively softer economic fields, mostly in urban India's vast unorganized or "informal" economy, in fields such as small or petty businesses, service assistants or other odd jobs in with the bigger companies or transport agencies. Countless numbers of them are employed in the new business economy of supplying goods and services to middle-class and upper-middle-class homes.

Quite like the consumption-driven middle class, this category of workers has also largely grown during the post-liberalization period. They have grown along with the expanding urban economy. They aspire to a place in the Indian growth story and hope to eventually climb up within the private economy. However, their realities remain precarious. Many of them are first-generation young migrants from villages or small towns and relatively less developed pockets of the country. Significant proportions of them remained employed in the informal sector or in an informal/insecure mode. This is the process we are witnessing in Laos today and which we describe in more detail in Chapter 3.

These migrants stay in pooled accommodations, often shared between five or six people. They eat at small roadside eateries and buy clothes and products that are imitations of established brands. Some who are middle-aged live in crammed apartments, having left their families in their native hinterland, and lead lives of forced bachelorhood. Those bring their families along live in irregular/unauthorized urban settlements or in lower-income group quarters in the urban peripheries. The rents they pay for their accommodations far exceed what they can afford. They travel long distances to their jobs. Their living conditions further deteriorate with the gradual and steady withdrawal of the state and the entry of private players as providers of water, electricity, transport and other basic amenities. The most prized possessions of those better-off in this class are invariably a two-wheeler, a "smart" cell phone and, occasionally, a laptop. For the young in this category, the internet, films and occasional strolls in the malls are the only sources of leisure.

Pinned down between the self-image and aspiration of being middle class on the one hand and the social and economic realities that accompany low-income groups in urban centers on the other, they almost always live in a state of anxiety, struggling between the needs of supporting their families, paying educational fees for their children's second- or third-grade private English-medium schools and maintaining the appearance of not being poor. This creates a self-constructed space where they sway between conformity and bitterness with regards to the larger social and economic systems, the political arrangements and choices they make for themselves and their families. Quite like their personal lives, their politics are also unpredictable. While this "neo-middle class", comparable to the Brazilian batalhadores, is indeed an unstable social, economic and political formation, its presence is functional for the hegemonic project of the Indian middle class, particularly in the context of widespread inequalities given its relatively small size in proportional terms.

Processes of middle-class consolidation in countries of Western Europe during the twentieth century were accompanied by institutionalization of a new language of citizenship. Even when economic disparities persisted, middle-class identification brought about a sense of commonness and homogeneity. Middle-class expansion implied the dissolution of the traditional hierarchies of status and rank and an advent of new notions of citizenship based on ideas of equality, fraternity and fairness. Even when differences of ethnicity, race or gender did not go away, the growing identification with being middle-class also implied an acceptance of a democratic public where nearly everyone could participate as equal members of the national political community. The Indian experience has so far been quite different.

Conclusion

According to a report published in 2016, India ranked second in the world in the index of inequality of wealth. The only other country that is more unequal, according to this report, is the former socialist country of Russia. As has happened in most parts of the world, economic inequalities have grown in India since the 1990s, with the unleashing of neoliberal economic reforms that also accelerated India's pace of economic growth. The nature of inequalities has changed as well, with much greater value being placed on urban-industrial and global capital. Even though a majority of Indians continue to be employed, part- or full-time, in the agrarian economy, it no longer seems to be shaping the structure of domination in the country.

However, these inequalities of wealth and capital are not socially colorless, emanating from an open and unbiased structure of opportunities where all citizens compete and only those with "merit" succeed and move ahead. Caste and other ascriptive identities continue to matter. Gender is an obvious marker of discrimination and bias. Similarly, religious community and diversity of ethnic identities also shape opportunity structures in the emerging economy of India. Further research on inequality must focus on the intersections of such qualitative processes and patterns.

Notes

1   The Indian team included Suraj Beri, Ishwari Bhattarai, Simin Fadaee and Andrea Silva.
2   'The Struggle for Equality in India'. See online: www.foreignaffairs.com/articles/asia/1962-07-01/struggle-equality-india. Accessed 23 December 2016.
3   A good example in this context is that of Sikhism in Punjab. The Sikh Gurus not only criticized Brahmanical values but also promoted institutions like *langar* (community kitchen and eating together) and *sangat*, congregational devotion (see McLeod 2000; Singh and Fenech 2014).
4   For a summary of this debate see Alice Thorner's review paper (Thorner 1982).
5   Estimates of its proportion in the total population of India vary a lot, from a meagre 5 per cent to 25 or 30 per cent (see Jodhka and Prakash 2016: 104–39).
6   "Macaulay's Minute on Education, February 2, 1835", Available at http://home.iitk.ac.in/~hcverma/Article/Macaulay-Minutes.pdf. Accessed 8 August 2014.
7   The OBCs are communities other than those listed as Scheduled Castes and they generally enjoy better status than the ex-untouchable communities (the SCs).
8   Election Manifesto of BhartiyaJanata Party for 2014 General Elections; available at www.bjp.org/images/pdf_2014/full_manifesto_english_07.04.2014.pdf. Accessed on 7 March 2015.

6 Capitalism and inequality on a global scale

In this chapter, we wish to summarize the findings of our country studies and relate them to the increasingly global structures and flows of capitalism. The main idea is to redirect research on inequality from capitalism to domination. We argue that capitalism is a particular system of domination that transforms earlier structures of domination or social hierarchies by converting the levels of these hierarchies into classes. The reproduction of the order of domination in capitalism has to take place via the economy, but the academic and popular focus on the economy makes the order of domination invisible and thereby contributes to its perpetuation.

The entire structure of domination comprises the hierarchy of classes as well as precapitalist sociocultures and dimensions of inequality. We argue that all of these inequalities function in a similar way, namely through symbolic classification. These inequalities are only reproduced if they appear as natural, legitimate and morally correct. Capitalism is based on symbolic liberalism, which declares all people as equal. Inequality would be illegitimate if it did not appear as a result of a fair competition and if its roots in an order of domination were visible. Our book seeks to contribute to making them visible.

The first part of the chapter briefly summarizes some of the points we made with regard to inequality in Brazil, Germany, India and Laos and draws a comparison between them. The idea is not only to pin down what is particular and what is general but also to complement the findings in such a way that a more encompassing view of inequality emerges. The second section of the chapter attempts to establish some theoretical conclusions on the basis of the comparison. In the final part, we will present preliminary ideas about the global structure of inequality and its connections to capitalism.

Comparison

We have constructed the country studies in previous chapters in such a way that they are both very different from each other and complement one another. The countries are from four world regions, differ greatly in size and in GDP per capita, represent different positions in the colonial and the present world order, have significantly different economic and political structures, experienced the capitalist transformation in different phases in the past and have extremely different precapitalist histories. We found that all four countries have developed similar class structures, which can be explained by a combination of tradition lines, distribution of capital, class culture and symbolic dividing lines. A significant part of the explanation for the similarity is that class has a particular relation to labor. In spite of these similarities, the precise configurations of the classes, the persisting structures of precapitalist inequalities and the habitus types differ vastly between the countries.

The chapter on Germany focuses on the notion and operationalization of class. We discovered three dividing lines, which are similar to those in Brazil and differ a bit from those in India and Laos. In all countries, the dividing lines contribute to the existence of social classes that are reproduced over many generations. Each class is mostly defined by its relation to labor. We call the four classes in Germany marginalized, fighters, established and aloof. The marginalized remain excluded from many sections of society, especially a stable and well-paid profession. They dispose of a small total volume of capital. The fighters are the core of society and form the bulk of the laboring population. The class of fighters consists of two tradition lines, one rooted in the old working class and one in the petty bourgeoisie. We can distinguish between aspiring and defensive fighters. The established carry out the leading functions and dispose of a large total amount of capital. The aloof are aloof in the sense that they are virtually separated from the rest of society and especially from labor. They form the dominant class.

The classes have different access to economic capital and labor. They are reproduced via the recruitment for hierarchically structured functions in the division of work in the widest sense. Each class has its own culture, habitus and life-worlds. As tradition lines, classes are not only defined by their capital but also by habitus and symbolic systems. Since their reproduction is mediated by the spheres of social practice, their cultures and the habitus forms have blurry edges. The habitus does not fully correspond to class.

The chapter on Laos tried to show how social classes emerge from precapitalist hierarchies as tradition lines. It also demonstrated that colonial, socialist and even precolonial social structures persist as sociocultures underneath the capitalist class structure. The social structure of Laos is changing rapidly but the precapitalist sociocultures persist and still inform the majority of structures and habitus. We discerned three sociocultures: *baan-muang*, socialism and capitalism. Within the first, there is a hierarchy of ethnic minorities, peasants in a difficult environment, peasants in a good environment, urban *muang* population and the nobility. Within the socialist socioculture, we can distinguish between village cadres, administration, leading cadres and party leadership. Within the socialist socioculture, there is much greater social mobility than in the other two sociocultures. The capitalist hierarchy comprises the marginalized class, the working class, commercial farmers and traders, the new urban middle class and the capitalists.

The older sociocultures slowly transform into a capitalist socioculture but the social groups tend to remain on their level of the social hierarchy. Subsistence peasants, who do not remain peasants, either become commercial farmers or agricultural laborers or they migrate into the towns. The small *muang* group transforms into the new urban middle class. The *muang* and the socialist elites begin to engage in business and become capitalists. Chinese and Vietnamese reappear – partly in their colonial role as businesspeople but also as farmers, laborers and petty traders. Laos is much more heterogeneous than Germany, as it is undergoing a rapid capitalist transformation. This entails a persistence of precapitalist habitus forms and hierarchies. We only found four habitus types in Laos, as opposed to six in Germany. These types also differ from each other significantly.

The Lao class structure differs from that in countries with a longer capitalist past, such as Germany and Brazil. The new urban middle class in Laos comprises professional groups that would be much better off in other countries and that would form an established class. In contrast, a petty bourgeoisie or middle class of the Western type does not exist in Laos. Its place is taken by the commercial farmers and traders, who in turn do not really form significant groups, let alone a class, in other countries. Finally, the other four classes are much smaller in Laos than in Germany.

Brazil, like Germany, has a long history of capitalism and a cemented class structure. Like Laos and in contrast to Germany, it was constructed by colonial rule. Contrary to India and Laos, not the entire population was declared equal upon gaining independence, as slaves, women and ethnic minorities only gained full citizenship over time. These inequalities persist up to this day and inform the Brazilian social structure. In these regards, Brazil has more in common with the US than with India, even though it shares many structural features of inequality with South Asia.

We found four classes in Brazil. This appears to match the German structure but a closer look reveals that the order of classes and their sizes are different. While dominant and marginalized classes of Germany and Brazil can be compared to some degree, the lower-middle class in Brazil does not exist in Germany, while the Brazilian upper-middle class comprises both of the classes that would be fighters and established in Germany. While the Brazilian ralé estrutural comprises up to 40 percent of the population, the German marginalized amount to half of that. The Brazilian middle class comprises only around 25 percent of the population, while the two German middle classes reach a total of almost 80 percent. We can trace the ralé estrutural and the batalhadores to the descendants of the slaves, the middle class to the administrators and the dominant class to the colonial rulers and landowners.

Because the Brazilian class structure emerged historically out of the hierarchy of a slave-holding society, its internal configuration and composition differs greatly from that of Germany and Laos. However, all three societies are developing similar dividing lines between the classes, namely the lines of dignity, expressivity and aloofness. In Laos, these lines are not yet very pervasive, while even in Brazil and Germany they do not entirely explain the class structure, as the Brazilian middle class and the German fighter class both comprise two tradition lines and habitus groups that do not fully correspond to the order of classes.

Despite significant regional, historical and cultural differences, the patterns of change and manifestations of inequality are surprisingly similar in the case of India as well. We have analyzed the Indian case and its experience of social, economic and political transformation through an empirical exploration into the dynamics of caste and class. Even though the orientalist and colonial knowledge systems constructed social hierarchies in India as being a peculiar or exceptional feature of the local culture of the Hindus, a closer look at the concept of caste also suggests that it has the classic features of what we have described in this book as symbolic classification and dividing lines. It is in the Indian case that the line of dignity (which corresponds to the line of pollution in the ideal-typical caste system) finds resonance, perhaps more than anywhere else in the world. As is evident from our other cases, Indian society has perhaps never been all that unique.

As in other countries of the global South (such as Brazil and Laos), the economy, politics and social arrangements in India have undergone profound changes over the past century and more. The introduction of modern industrial technology, systems of enumerations and Western-style administrative structures initiated by the colonial rulers have had far-reaching implications and in many ways paved the way for significant transformations of the region. Independence from colonial rule in 1947 and massive investments by the post-colonial state system in building the physical and industrial infrastructure further accelerated the process of capitalist development. The Indian state also adopted a democratic Constitution and initiated a system of affirmative action to enable those located at the margins to integrate. Agriculture, industry and a modern service system grew rapidly. The pace of this growth saw further acceleration after the introduction of neoliberal economic reforms in the early 1990s. A new narrative of middle-classness and individual mobility also acquired a hegemonic value around the same time. The tradition-bound ascriptive hierarchies were to give way to a newer classification based on individual achievement.

On the ground, however, the inequalities of caste have persisted. Even as the middle class grows, its internal hierarchy tends to closely overlap with the earlier hierarchies of caste. The pull of urbanization draws the ex-untouchables out of the villages, into the rapidly growing cities and cosmopolitan centers. However, a large majority of them tend to find space only at the lowest end of employment in the urban economy, with no security, no dignity and no visibility. The other end of the urban economy also shows similar patterns with top-end corporate jobs having been virtually a monopoly of those from the traditionally privileged or "upper" caste background. Not that nothing has changed. Some from the lower rungs have moved up and not everyone from the upper castes is rich and powerful, but the division and inequalities are not simply a consequence of individual merit and achievement.

It seems that the structure of four classes and three dividing lines that we found in Germany is emerging in all capitalist countries. However, the classes will not comprise the same tradition lines or cultures and will not have the same sizes everywhere. It is interesting to note that Karl Marx already assumed the existence of almost the same four classes in the *Communist Manifesto* (1964). As is well-known, he distinguished capital and labor but he also argued that capitalism produces the "reserve army" or even a class of "superfluous" nonlaborers. And he added that between capital and labor, a middle class of shopkeepers, craftspeople, employees and privileged laborers partly persists from feudal times and partly develops with capitalism. Tracing the fate of these classes over one and a half centuries, we realize that Marx's "old middle class" has split into the defensive fighters and the established class in contemporary Germany, while the class of laborers has transformed into the tradition line of the aspiring fighters. Theodor Geiger (1932) discovered five tradition lines, which resemble our five tradition lines in Germany after the First World War, and already diagnosed the descent of the old middle class.

Old middle classes do exist in Brazil, India and Laos as well but they are located in a very different social order and division of labor. Similarly, the new middle classes in these countries do not clearly divide the established from the fighters. Finally, India and Laos host a rural middle class, which has ceased to exist in Brazil and Germany. These differences will not disappear entirely in the near future, as they are part of the historical heritage and are reproduced both by habitus and by the (international) division of labor.

The habitus types we established in Brazil, Germany and Laos differ even more from each other, since they are more closely associated with the sociocultures. The strong continuity of very unequal structures in Brazil leads to a significant congruence of habitus and class. This is not at all the case in Germany and Laos, albeit for different reasons. Habitus types in Laos differ mainly in their roots in different sociocultures and to some (lesser) degree in their hierarchical position. Habitus types in Germany have their roots in the classes but extend beyond class lines because of the seemingly more egalitarian social practice. Both in Brazil and in Germany, each class contains a more culture-oriented and a more money-oriented pole, just as Bourdieu (1984) observed in France. This opposition cannot be detected in Laos. However, cultural capital is much more relevant for the class position in Germany than in the other three countries. This, of course, is related to Germany's strong specialization on technology within the international division of labor.

Even though the habitus types differ hugely between the countries, we have found the characteristic of self-determination, or autonomy, to be a marker of upper classes (and its lack to be a marker of lower classes) in all four countries. The oppositions of creative and disciplined as well as of active and passive seem to be emerging as relevant within the capitalist socioculture, too. These traits in turn are related to class on the one hand and to cultural capital on the other hand.

Mechanisms of inequality

There is no doubt that the total amount of all types of capital and the dispositions incorporated by the habitus are two of the core principles of stratification in capitalist societies. As we have shown, they even work in a similar way and structure, as Bourdieu (1984) has argued with regard to France in the late 1960s. However, we have added that the distribution of capital and habitus does not explain inequality, not even in an old capitalist society, such as France. We need to study the emergence and reproduction of classes as tradition lines and we have to establish the dividing lines between them. In this section, we wish to demonstrate that the dividing lines, in turn, are constituted by symbolic classification. This is a process of constructing, evaluating and reproducing moral characteristics of entire groups of people, which are thereby produced as groups in a hierarchy and virtual communities.

We have seen that classes in capitalist societies tend to be defined by three dividing lines. The most relevant line is that between "worthy" and "unworthy" people – that is, those who contribute something to society and those who do not. The "worthy" people live above an invisible line of dignity. They are divided by a second line, which is that of "sensibility" or "expressivity", into an upper class of savvy people equipped for the leading functions in society and a lower class of the mere laborers, the "workhorses". A tiny class aloof from any classification and competition sits above the hierarchy. Aloofness constitutes the third dividing line. The dividing lines between the classes are incorporated actively and passively. They are used to give or deny access to whatever function in society, to assess people, to choose a marriage partner and to guide one's own actions.

However, class does not explain all inequality, even in a capitalist society. As is evident from this exposition of symbolic classification in the present-day capitalist societies, including those in the West, inequality is not simply about disparities of income and wealth, resulting from unequal achievements of individuals, given their skills, merit and dispositions. The contemporary mechanisms of inequality and its reproduction in everyday life is also not explainable by the Marxist or the Bourdieuan notions of the accumulation of whatever kinds of capital. This is because the reproduction of such inequalities has something ascriptive or "ethnic" about it. Groups-based differences and valuations are passed on from generation to generation.

Max Weber (1972) described these differences as status groups and he used such a hierarchical notion of status group quite rightly for the caste system, which is a system of ascriptive hierarchies and vertical ethnic formations (see Jodhka 2016). He also pointed to the fact that status groups are not peculiar to India. However, they are not as vulnerable to "modernization" as he thought. They persist underneath class and they form a component of class. This renders Weber's concept of economic class much more irrelevant for understanding contemporary society than the concepts of social class and status group.

The idea of modernization and the functionalist notion of evolution compel us to either not see such realities around us (as in the case of most societies of the contemporary West) or see them as mere cases of aberrations and deviations. Against this dominant common sense, we argue that caste-like differences and hierarchies are constitutive of all capitalist societies. In many ways, it is this association of economic inequality with some notions of ascription, assumed or real, that make such differences of income and wealth as social, political and cultural *inequality*. Quite like caste, all these systems of inequality find their legitimacy in the prevailing dominant culture. This could be, on the extreme, Hindu rituals or, on the other, the modernist notion of merit and the illusion of endless opportunities or possibilities of achievement for an able and hard-working individual. It other words, the category of caste perhaps describes inequality better than the popular notion of class.

Structures of global domination

Symbolic classification extends to the global level and partly explains the hierarchy of nation-states and their citizens. However, we have to link the symbolic dimension to the structures of domination and capitalism, just as we have done in the country studies. The contemporary world order is a transformation of the colonial world, the inequalities of which partly persist and partly have been transformed into capitalist structures. On the global level, as on the national, an egalitarian and meritocratic discourse is coupled with a legitimation that we have called symbolic racism. All of us are influenced to some degree or another by modernization theory, which is the capitalist transformation of colonial evolutionism. We tend to view the order of nation-states as a result of their (capitalist) development.

Modernization theory depicts societies in the global South as deficient realizations of the Northatlantic model. Niklas Luhmann (1995), for example, distinguished between "decent" and "corrupt" societies after his visit to Brazil, thereby idealizing Northatlantic societies. Variants of this idea are deeply incorporated in our common sense and in the foundations of social science. These range from notions of desirable aspirations, modes of individual behavior and notions of "good life" to larger frames of organizing social, economic and political life. We think of economically less developed societies, which need to implement reforms in order to reach such standards of social organization and institutions, and of developed societies, which have by and large met or even elaborated these standards. Closely connected to this idea is the interpretation of "underdeveloped" societies as corrupt, inefficient, undemocratic and somehow incomplete, while their citizens are regarded as untrustworthy and undisciplined. Good examples beyond our own common sense would be: the depiction of Mexicans in American movies; the financial country ratings by agencies like Moody's; and the still popular notions of India as a land of snake charmers, Maharajas and a never-changing caste system. This idea implies that inequality in Northatlantic societies is either a transient phenomenon (Kuznets 1955) or a desirable result of a fully developed market economy (Friedman 1962).

The explicit or implicit argument claims that capitalism in Northatlantic societies is decent and more developed, while all other arrangements are classified as corrupt and deficient. This view of the world was convincing as long as Europe ruled the colonial world and as long as the United States was the world's superpower. It is less convincing since Singapore has achieved the highest GDP per capita and China the largest volume of trade as well as the second-largest GDP. It is quite obvious that these countries have institutional configurations that differ significantly from those of Europe and the US and will continue to do so for some time to come. However, the general framework of modernization theory still prevails. All rankings – from the worthiness of credit to corruption to human development – largely translate the colonial order into an order of development and modernization.

The reason for this persistence is its direct link to the order of nation-states. Our argument in the section on migration to Germany refers to this order. Flows and outcomes of migration are indicators for the order of states. The classification of a migrant depends on the ranking of his or her country of origin in the global order of states (Grosfoguel 2004). This is significant for inequality between nation-states and between individuals. Whether you are allowed to stay in a nation-state, whether you are allowed to apply for formal wage-labor, whether your educational degree is recognized and whether you find a job matching that degree largely depends on the relation of your country of origin and the receiving country. This relation is partly determined on the basis of modernization theory. The rankings by the UN, think tanks and governments use such indicators as GDP, development of technology, Western education system, bio-medicine, Western democracy and corruption. These are the indicators of modernization theory.

However, the order of states determines the outcome of migration only to a certain degree. A university professor and a rural laborer from the same country of origin will occupy very different social positions after migration. Their positions, to a large degree, depend on their capital and habitus. Determining inequality on a global scale would mean finding a common measure for capital and habitus across nation-states. Anja Weiß (2017) has come up with a concept corresponding to this need for a common measure. She assesses the possibility of employing one's capital and habitus in different national contexts as "sociospatial autonomy". This concept bridges the gap that exists in Bourdieu's theory between conditions and practice, operates on a global scale and includes the aspect of space. Sociospatial autonomy means the ability to move anywhere without jeopardizing one's social position. The maximum sociospatial autonomy would be the access to all valuable functions and positions in society.

The concept of sociospatial autonomy solves many problems of global inequality research and includes several insights, namely the order of nation-states, the divergence between the national and the global distribution of capital and habitus, the inequality between different places and the inequality associated with migration. We consider Weiß's concept a milestone in the debates on the topic and would continue to refer to it.

However, we need to add at least two dimensions to the concept. First, economic capital becomes increasingly detached from place today. Second, the world has not become fully globalized. The nation-state continues to be the most important framework both for inequality and for sociological research. This entails a contradiction in and for the position of the dominant classes.

Their social position is tied to the nation-state and can only be reproduced within it; at the same time, their actions and interests are increasingly global.

The national roots of the dominant classes give them less sociospatial autonomy than the established classes. A university professor can use his or her capital in most nation-states to a similar degree and occupies a similar social position before and after migration. This is often not the case for members of the dominant class. Even a Mittal or Tata does not automatically become a member of the British dominant class after migrating to London. And even if a Kennedy became member of the Indian dominant class after migrating to India – which is questionable – his global position and influence would suffer. For this reason, we see little international migration among the top end of society (Hartmann 2007).

This issue is linked to the deeper historical contradiction between capitalism and the nation-state. The European nation-state was closely linked to colonialism, which in turn implied the global expansion of (Western) capitalism. Francis Bacon was not only one of the founders of Western science but also lord-chancellor of England and the founding member of several colonial companies. The nation-state in Europe developed technology, an efficient division of labor and administration in the interior, at the same time as colonial expansion and global reproduction of capital. All of this happened under the leadership of the dominant classes in the European nation-states. The rest of the world was either forced to adopt this model or the dominant classes in the newly independent countries of the former colonial world adopted it voluntarily to their own advantage. The world today is divided into nation-states, which have very similar institutions, from the economy to culture to politics. All of them retain their historical peculiarities, as we have argued in this book, and all of them are limited by their national borders.

The dominant classes consist mainly of capitalists who act globally and strive for economic and political power on a global scale. Their means of action are multinational corporations, international financial institutions and tax havens. All of these are limited in their scope by nation-states and their regulations – even if these states were founded to pursue the interests of the dominant classes and are still very much influenced by them. The interests of the dominant class and its nation-state are not necessarily identical but the dominant class can reproduce its social position and secure its interests only by means of the state. Furthermore, the interests of the different national dominant classes may collide. The dominant classes do not pursue one common agenda of global domination.

The increasingly homogeneous order of standardized nation-states is complemented by an increasingly identical order of classes. Each class has a particular function in the structure of domination and a symbolic relation to labor: the dominant class monopolizes capital, the established class (functional elites) manages society, the middle class labors, and the marginalized are the "reserve army" and the "other" who creates fear. We argue that this structure is reproduced within each nation-state effectively if it remains invisible and unconscious, as each class is best equipped for its social functions. This partly explains the idea of sociospatial autonomy.

The idea also points to the order of nation-states. The states are not only standardized, but they also form a hierarchy. This hierarchy, rooted in the colonial order and partly explained by it, is perpetuated by modernization theory, symbolic racism and the global distribution of capital. To understand this hierarchy and the lacking sociospatial autonomy of the dominant class, we need to take a closer look at the dominant class and its relation to global capital and the nation-state.

The basic fact about the dominant class in capitalism leads us back to the first paragraphs of this book and Thomas Piketty: it is the extreme concentration of economic capital. However, at this point, we need to deconstruct the notion of economic capital, which is based on symbolic liberalism. The concentration of capital is portrayed as a result of competition. We argue that it is the foundation of capitalism.

In this regard, we also need to point to the ambiguity in the term "economic capital", which has been overlooked by Bourdieu and is exploited by symbolic liberalism. More than 99.9 percent of the world population do not own any means that can be used as *capital*, even if they own goods or money. The overwhelming majority of human beings owns very little, and those who do own something consume what they own: their private home, their car, their clothes, their luxury goods. If we specify who actually owns economic capital that can be invested for profit, we understand Piketty's claim of an extreme concentration of capital in the hands of a very few. And we can give a more accurate estimate of their number.

The dominant class disposes of around half of global wealth, which means almost the entire economic capital in the strict sense. It maintains its position and coherence not only by means of economic capital but at least to the same degree by social capital. According to the Global Wealth Report, 34 million people, less than 1 percent of the world population, own wealth of more than one million USD (Stierli et al. 2015: 20). In the US, it is 5 percent of the population, in Germany 2 percent and in Laos a handful of individuals. Western Europe, North America, Japan and Australia host 83 percent of the world's millionaires. Of the millionaires, only four million own wealth worth more than five million USD and 124.000 more than fifty million. Of these latter, 50 percent live in North America and 24 percent in Europe. If we include all millionaires in the group of potential capitalists, we reach a number of 0.5 percent of the world population – half of the famous "one percent" (Piketty 2014). However, if we exclude those with wealth in the range of less than, say, five million USD, we are left with 0.05 percent of the world population as actual capitalists, most of whom are citizens of Europe and North America. Up to 2 percent of the US population and 0.5 percent of the German population are capitalists and possibly members of the dominant classes. These 0.05 percent of the world population own virtually all the economic capital in the strict sense. The rest of the population competes for means of consumption but, in most cases, not for capital. Both groups are playing a different game.

Vitali et al. (2011) have studied the network of transnational corporations (TNC) and their ownership. They identified 43,000 TNCs. 15,491 of them have mutual ownership ties and 295 form the core of the network. Within the core, three-quarters of the corporations' shares are held by other TNCs of the core. 147 of these hold 40 percent of all TNC shares. The authors conclude that these 147 TNCs control the global economy and themselves. Actually, they control about a quarter of global GDP. The nation-states account for a huge chunk, which we estimate at 40 percent. The largest corporations are mostly owned by each other and by financial institutions. This means that global production for consumption is controlled by fewer than two hundred private companies and a smaller number of large nation-states. Both the states and the corporations are mostly located in Western Europe and North America (Vitali et al. 2011: 26).

If the most powerful TNCs own each other, does nobody own anything? Private investors appear less and less as the major shareholders of these large companies. But they invest via financial institutions. Some of these institutions require a minimum investment of up to one billion USD. This restricts the circle of possible investors to a very small group – which is recruited overwhelmingly from the world's dominant classes. As financial investors, the dominant classes form a global entity. However, they still do not form a global class, as their position is reproduced only within the nation-state.

The nation-states are not mere instruments of the dominant classes but their relationship explains a large part of global inequality. Half of the world's dominant class are citizens of North America and a quarter are citizens of Western Europe. The dominant class of the US alone is in a position of unique global economic power. It is in an even better political position than other dominant classes, because its interests converge with those of the nation-state US. Both strive for global domination. Interests of dominant classes and states tend to diverge in the smaller countries, since the global action of the dominant class is counteracted by a nationalist agenda of the state.

We saw a similar picture with the rise of the North Italian city states (which was ended by the religious wars and the expansion of the pope's power) and with the rise of England as a colonial power. State and dominant class pursued the same agenda of global expansion. We are seeing a similar match of interests in contemporary China and in Russia. The Chinese state will be able to rival the US to the degree that it can mobilize its dominant class and global capital, while the Chinese dominant class depends on the Chinese state in order to grow.

The idea of sociospatial autonomy does not explain global inequality – but it is relevant for around 99.9 percent of the world population. The dominant classes comprise no more than 0.1 of humanity. But we could say that the entire spectacle of capitalism serves only their interests. The rest of the population consists of – actual or aspiring – laborers. The dominant classes are structured into a hierarchy that corresponds to the hierarchy of nation-states and to sheer economic power. The relation of dominant class and nation-state exerts a key influence on the position of the state in the hierarchy of states.

The dominant class in each nation-state has to reproduce its social position by accumulating economic capital, which has to be invested in a profitable way, often against the interests of the nation-state. In order to reproduce its social position, it also has to accumulate social capital, which is strongly focused on the nation-state. Cultural capital is less relevant but also plays an important role in management and family strategy to make the right investment decisions. All three types of capital are also used to directly influence the nation-state. One could also talk of political capital. Members of the dominant class invest in corruption, party donations, lobbies, think tanks, media ownership and personal networks in order to influence policies. These are mostly national policies. Supranational organizations are lobbied mainly by corporations and organizations, but in some regards they are subject to private manipulations as well.

Symbolic capital seems not as relevant in the dominant class as in the established class but this is only true for the relation of this class with the rest of society. The main characteristic of this class, according to our research, is its aloofness. There is almost no direct interaction between this class and the rest. The members of the dominant class do not need to prove themselves and therefore do not need symbolic capital. However, symbolic capital is crucial to maintain membership of the class itself.

One of the most important issues in these coming years is the relation between globalism and nationalism within the dominant class – which is also about international cooperation and competition between national dominant classes. In this framework, the key question for the coming years is the actual globalization of the dominant classes. As capitalists, they are already entirely globalized. But their domination is limited to their respective nation-state. In both dimensions, the families and alliances within this class are global competitors and need national development.

Conclusion

This chapter has compared the results of our four country studies in order to establish more general conclusions. The conclusions concern the relation between class and socioculture, the mechanism of the production and reproduction of inequality, and the problem of global inequality. Our conclusions regarding these three issues are preliminary, since they are based only on four countries. However, our research has been original and largely qualitative. It is not based on dubious secondhand data or newspaper articles, in contrast to most "research" on inequality. Therefore, the results presented in this chapter will certainly have to be amended and corrected in many ways but we suggest that they are a first step in an endeavor which will require a lot more empirical group work.

The main result concerning the relation between class and socioculture in capitalist societies is the emergence of a four-class structure based on the dividing lines of dignity, expressivity and aloofness. At the same time, earlier sociocultures persist and inform the actual configuration of the classes. We have found that the dividing lines between the classes become more solid with time and that the marginalized classes are larger in countries with a strong and unequal colonial heritage.

With regard to production and reproduction of inequality, we found that symbolic classification on the basis of inherited inequalities is the key mechanism. Caste is the prime example and a good case study of this mechanism. In contrast to the (Orientalist) literature on India, caste is not a singular and especially exotic institution of an isolated world region but it makes visible those processes and structures that are less visible in other configurations of inequality.

Finally, we have argued that capitalism is an order of global domination that is based on a combination of dominant classes and nation-states. The institution of the nation-state was key in the expansion of (Western) capitalism and in the attempts of dominant classes to achieve supraregional and later global domination. At the same time, this institution limits the power of dominant classes – except for those in the dominant nation-state. Today, there is no single dominant nation-state any more. The multicentric world has returned (Nederveen Pieterse and Rehbein 2008). This makes the global order of nation-states and thereby global inequality even more complex and difficult to understand.

Conclusion

This book has tried to understand social inequality in capitalist societies based on the empirical study of four countries from four world regions. The empirical study drew on existing theories, conceptual frameworks and methodologies but had to extend and modify them to include diverse societies from the global South. To our knowledge, no such comparison based on original empirical material gathered in the local languages, has ever been undertaken. Therefore, our research necessitated some conceptual and theoretical work, the results of which we will summarize in this conclusion before briefly reviewing the empirical results and drawing some political conclusions.

In this book, we interpret phenomena of the social world from the perspective of meaningful practice. Human actions are imbued with meaning. We follow Cassirer (1997) in his use of the term "symbol" to grasp the aspect of meaning. We argue that human practice is always symbolically mediated and that the understanding of this process is the key to understanding society. From this perspective, the symbolic mediation of power is the structural root of inequality, which is domination. Power is understood as the impersonal possibility of influencing the social definition and practice of life.

Following Wittgenstein, we have analyzed meaningful practice into forms of life. According to him, forms of life extend to a highly variable number of people. While some contexts are limited to small in-groups, others seem to comprise the entirety of humankind. Wittgenstein (1989) argued that this is the precondition for understanding people from other societies, cultures and language families. This also implies that there are some components of the habitus that are shared by many people, and others by very few.

In order to understand the complex web of differences and similarities between the countries, we have distinguished, like Bourdieu (1984), between two modes of existence of the social, namely objective and subjective. Following Weber (2011), we have analyzed each mode into several layers of meaning according to the reach that each layer has within (global) society. The objective mode of society comprises structures, institutions, physical existence and so on. The subjective mode refers to the embodied patterns of acting, thinking, perceiving, etc.

The objective layers of meaning can be analyzed into culture in the widest sense – society, socioculture, institution and social environment – and the subjective layers into humanity, agents or groups, habitus and ethos. By culture, we mean the general organization of practices in the anthropological sense. Ethos refers to the orientation of practice by a social group. We add agents, because collectives can act. Even if they act through persons, these appear as organs of the collective and not as individuals.

The basic layer is common to everyone, whereas the top layer is individual and not fully determined by biology and society. This means that a sociological study deals only with the intermediate layers. This is in fact what Bourdieu does, and we follow him in this book. It implies, too, that he was misguided in his endeavor to deduce the top layers from lower layers, as the preconditioning is not a full determination and does not allow for a deduction. The preconditioning, though, entails statistical correlations and allows for an explanation. Finally, Bourdieu used the concept of habitus only for the intermediate layers, precisely because it expresses social differences. Where the form of life is so basic and all-encompassing that few social differences emerge, the concept makes little sense.

In our analysis of capitalist societies, we drew on Bourdieu by studying the unequal distribution of all relevant forms of capital and valuable habitus traits. We had to go beyond this framework in view of the historical dimension and in view of the general concept of symbolically mediated practice outlined earlier. Bourdieu disregarded the historical dimension of sociocultures and the coexistence of different layers of social structure within one society. The neglect has no systematic reasons but arises instead out of the belief in modernization theory and the apparent uniformity of a Western society. However, all contemporary societies are products of a long history and the capitalist transformation. Current social groups, cultures and classes are rooted in earlier hierarchies. We refer to the continuities of these hierarchical segments as tradition lines. Each tradition line is subject to social change and transformation. While most traditions are passed on from one generation to the next, some are transformed, others are forgotten or lost and new ones emerge. Large-scale transformations can lead to actual breaks within a tradition line.

The segmentation of tradition lines according to different sociocultures gives rise to distinct social environments, which we call milieus, a term first introduced by Emile Durkheim (1997). While Bourdieu's concept of class sorts people with similar resources into groups, the concept of milieu refers to an impersonal context in which people will most likely operate for the majority of their lives. The milieu is the matrix in which a person acts, thinks, experiences and judges. The individual acquires abilities and inclinations within a society and within a certain milieu. Society's entire stock of inclinations forms the total amount of all acquirable inclinations, whereas the milieu confines this stock of inclinations to a particular section. Milieus are consequences of the transformation of a tradition line. This means that older milieus incorporate older social structures as sociocultures. It also implies that only stratified societies that have undergone at least one relatively recent transformation are differentiated into milieus.

None of the concepts introduced so far has to be confined to the framework of the nation-state. In fact, most social environments are either smaller or larger than the nation-state and even cross its borders. It is also important to note that the history of transformations does not constitute a linear evolution to supposedly higher forms. Most transformations contain both progressive and regressive elements as well as deviations. However, we have argued that the nation-state still is the most relevant entity in the capitalist world. Therefore, our study has focused on the comparison between nation-states, even though we introduced the global level in the final chapter of this book.

We argue that global inequality has to be interpreted as an order of global domination. This order is based on a combination of dominant classes and nation-states. The institution of the nation-state was key in the expansion of (Western) capitalism and in the attempts of dominant classes to achieve supra-regional and later global domination. At the same time, this institution limits the power of dominant classes – except for those in the dominant nation-state. The relation between dominant class and nation-state seems to be of key importance to understanding global inequality.

In terms of the internal structure of the four nation-states, we found that they comprise four or five classes and varying degrees of precapitalist inequalities. We estimate that a four-class structure based on the dividing lines of dignity, expressivity and aloofness will emerge in most states. At the same time, earlier sociocultures persist and inform the actual configuration of the classes. We have found that the dividing lines between the classes become more solid with time and that the marginalized classes are larger in countries with a strong and unequal colonial heritage. The dividing lines are constituted and reproduced by symbolic classification, which confers different moral values to classes of people. We have argued that this symbolic construction of inequality is the general mechanism establishing social inequality.

We would argue that inequalities between classes, genders, races, ethnicities and castes all function in a very similar way, namely through symbolic classification. We added that in capitalist societies, class becomes a more important form of inequality than the other dimensions. In order to illustrate this, we have studied the intersection of gender and class in Germany and Laos. Each class and each socioculture has its own configuration of gender inequality – but this relationship does not function the other way around. We make similar points with regard to migration to Germany, caste in India and ethnicity in Laos. However, no type of inequality can be reduced to class or subsumed under class. Just like the hierarchies of each socioculture, these earlier inequalities are partly transformed by capitalism, partly disappear and partly persist as they are.

Based on our preliminary findings and our theoretical considerations, we have attempted an operationalization of our approach that does justice to Wittgenstein's concept of forms of life. The operationalization is based on Wittgenstein's notion of family resemblance. The members of a family share many typical characteristics with each other but no two share all. Therefore, the characteristics cannot be subsumed under a set of axiomatic variables. We define classes as "social families" and establish them empirically on the basis of family resemblances. In the process, we applied an appropriate methodological tool, namely multiple correspondence analysis. This tool allows us to identify and weight the joint existence of social characteristics. Class position is not defined by a single indicator, such as profession or wealth, but by a combination of factors which have to be determined empirically.

Our research showed clear and insurmountable dividing lines in all four societies within the capitalist socioculture. This empirical result led us to explore the dividing lines and link them both to labor and to moral evaluation. Only in connection to this did we come up with the notion of class, as we introduce it in this book – as a tradition line reproducing itself via habitus and capital, allowing for little mobility across its boundaries and reconfirming the boundaries via symbolic classification. We argue that this notion of class advances our understanding of inequality in capitalist societies.

Our studies have revealed that some social mobility is possible across class lines. However, all the examples we found are related to a major social upheaval – either a violent one like war or revolution or a peaceful one by means of committed political intervention. We detected no substantial social mobility in Germany over the entire twentieth century except in the wake of the Second World War. Likewise, mobility in India seems to have been linked to the struggle for independence. But we see social mobility in India and Laos linked to the capitalist transformation. And social structure became fluid in Laos in the wake of the socialist revolution. Finally, the social measures of the Lula administration in Brazil targeting the marginalized class led to the emergence of a new class above the line of dignity.

The example of Brazil shows that political measures against social inequality are possible and can have a significant effect. But they have to go beyond economic capital and have to be sustained over generations. The Brazilian initiative against inequality is somewhat unique in its combination of economic assistance and education. This lifted nearly forty million Brazilians out of poverty. However, the effects may not last very much longer since the current government of Brazil has basically suspended the struggle against inequality. The class of the batalhadores may disappear again.

This situation is linked to the problem of symbolic inequality. The measures in Brazil included cultural capital but did not target symbolic racism. The batalhadores are still considered as unequal by the Brazilian middle class. Therefore, inequality was reproduced in spite of effective policies. And the class of the batalhadores never merged with the existing middle class. Any struggle against inequality has to include an outspoken and sufficiently sophisticated policy against symbolic racism.

Finally, social inequality will persist as long as capitalism persists. It can be alleviated by policies, but it will not disappear. We have argued that capitalism is a system of domination that focuses on the accumulation of economic capital, serves only the dominant class and seeks to make domination invisible by means of symbolic liberalism. We added that most studies of inequality contribute to this project and thereby help to sustain the particular shape that inequality takes in capitalist societies.

References

Abu-Lughod, Janet L. (1989) *Before European Hegemony: The World System, A.D. 1250–1350*, New York/Oxford: Oxford University Press

Ajit D., Han Donker, Ravi Saxena (2012) 'Corporate Boards in India: Blocked by Caste?,' *Economic and Political Weekly*, Vol. XLVII (31): 39-43

Arendt, Hannah (1958) *The Human Condition*, Chicago: University of Chicago Press

Bairy, Ramesh (2009) 'Brahmins in the Modern World: Association as Enunciation', *Contributions to Indian Sociology*, Vol. 43 (1): 89–120

Bardhan, Pranab (1984) *The Political Economy of Development in India*, Delhi: Oxford University Press

Bayard, Donn T. (ed.) (1984) *Southeast Asian Archaeology at the XV Pacific Science Congress: The Origins of Agriculture, Metallurgy, and the State in Mainland Southeast Asia*, Dunedin: University of Otago Press

Beck, Ulrich (1986) *Risikogesellschaft*, Frankfurt: Suhrkamp

Bellah, Robert N., Steven M. Tipton, William M. Sullivan, Richard Madsen, and Ann Swidler (1985) *Habits of the Heart: Individualism and Commitment in American Life*, Berkeley: University of California Press

Beteille, André (1974) *Studies in Agrarian Social Structure*, Delhi: Oxford University Press

Bohnsack, Ralf (2014; eighth edition) *Rekonstruktive Sozialforschung*, Opladen: Budrich

Bourdet, Yves (2000) *The Economics of Transition in Laos: From Socialism to ASEAN Integration*, Cheltenham: Elgar

Bourdieu, Pierre (1963) *Travail et travailleurs en Algérie*, La Hague: Editions Mouton

Bourdieu, Pierre (1984) *Distinction*, Cambridge, MA: Harvard University Press

Bourdieu, Pierre (1990) *The Logic of Practice*, Cambridge: Polity Press

Bourdieu, Pierre and Loïc Wacquant (1992) *An Invitation to Reflexive Anthropology*, Chicago: University of Chicago Press

Bourlet, Antoine (1906) 'Socialisme dans les hua-phan (Laos, Indo-Chine)', *Anthropos*, Vol. I: 521–8

Buarque, Sérgio (2001) *Raízes do Brasil*, São Paulo: Companhia das Letras

Cassirer, Ernst (1997) *Philosophie der symbolischen Formen*, Darmstadt: Wissenschaftliche Buchgesellschaft

Charsley, S.R. and G.K. Karanth (1998) *Dalits and State Action: The 'SCs' Challenging Untouchability: Dalit Initiative and Experience From Karnataka*, New Delhi: Sage

Chatterjee, Partha (1993) *The Nation and Its Fragments: Colonial and Postcolonial Histories*, Princeton: Princeton University Press

Ciotti, Manuela (2012) *Retro-modern India: Forging the Low Caste Self*, New Delhi: Routledge

Cohn, Bernard S. (1996) *Colonialism and Its Forms of Knowledge: The British in India*, Princeton: Princeton University Press

Condominas, Georges (1962) *Essai sur la société rurale de la région de Vientiane*, Vientiane (typescript)

Crenshaw, Kimberlé (1989) 'Demarginalizing the Intersection of Race and Sex', *University of Chicago Legal Forum*: 139–67

Da Matta, Roberto (1981) *Carnavais, malandros e heróis*, Rio de Janeiro: Zahar

Desai, A.R. (1948) *Social Background of Indian Nationalism*, Bombay: Popular Prakashan

Dirks, Nicholas (2001) *Castes of Mind: Colonialism and the Making of Modern India*, Princeton: Princeton University Press

Doré, Amphay (1980) *Le partage du Mekong*, Paris: Encre

Dumont, Louis (1971) *Homo Hierarchicus: The Caste System and Its Implications*, New Delhi: Oxford University Press

Durkheim, Emile (1997) *The Division of Labor in Society*, New York: Free Press

Embree, John F. (1969) 'Thailand – A Loosely Structured Social System', in Hans-Dieter Evers (ed.) *Loosely Structured Social Systems: Thailand in Comparative Perspective*, New Haven: Yale University Press: 3–15

Epprecht, Michael, Peter Messerli, Andreas Heiniman, Phonesaly Souksavath, Thiraka Chanthalanouvong, and Nicholas Minot (2008) *Geography of Poverty and Inequality in the Lao PDR*, Bern: Swiss National Center of Competence in Research

Evans, Grant (1990) *Lao Peasants Under Socialism*, New Haven: Yale University Press

Foucault, Michel (1977) *Discipline and Punish*, New York: Pantheon Books

Frank, André Gunder (1998) *ReOrient*, Berkeley: University of California Press

Friedman, Milton (1962) *Capitalism and Freedom*, Chicago: University of Chicago Press

Fuller, C.J. and Haripriya Narasimhan (2015) *Tamil Brahmans: The Making of a Middle-Class Caste*, New Delhi: Social Science Press

Gay, Bernard (1995) 'Notes sur le Laos sous le protectorat français (de 1893 à 1940)', in Nguyen The Anh and Alain Forest (eds.) *Notes sur la culture et la religion en Péninsule indochinoise – en hommage à Pierre-Bernard Lafont*, Paris: L'Harmattan: 227–41

Geiger, Theodor (1932) *Die soziale Schichtung des deutschen Volkes*, Stuttgart: Ferdinand Enke Verlag

Goffman, Erving (1979) *Gender Advertisements*, New York: Harper Collins

Goldthorpe, John H. (2007) *On Sociology*, Stanford: Stanford University Press

Grosfoguel, Ramón (2004) 'Race and Ethnicity or Racialized Ethnicities? Identities Within Global Coloniality', *Ethnicities*, Vol. 4: 315–36

Guha, Sumit (2013) *Beyond Caste Beyond Caste: Identity and Power in South Asia, Past and Present*, Leiden: Brill (Brill's Indological Library).

Gupta, Dipankar (2000) *Interrogating Caste: Understanding Hierarchy and Difference in Indian Society*, New Delhi: Penguin Books India

Guru, Gopal (2001) 'Dalit Middle Class Hangs in the Air', in Imtiaz Ahmad and Helmut Reifeld (eds.) *Middle Class Values in India and Western Europe*, New Delhi: Social Science Press: 141–51

Guru, Gopal (2012) 'Rise of the "Dalit Millionaire": A Low Intensity Spectacle', *Economic and Political Weekly*, Vol. 47 (50): 41–9

Halpern, Joel M. (1964) *Economy and Society in Laos* (Laos Project Paper), New Haven: Yale University Press

Hartmann, Michael (2007) *The Sociology of Elites*, London/New York: Routledge

Higham, Charles (1989) *The Archaeology of Mainland Southeast Asia*, Cambridge: Cambridge University Press

Hobbes, Thomas (1968) *Leviathan*, London: Pelican

Hobson, John M. (2004) *The Eastern Origins of Western Civilization*, Cambridge: Cambridge University Press

Ireson, Carol J. (1996) *Field, Forest, and Family: Women's Work and Power in Rural Laos*, Boulder: Westview Press

Iyer, Lakshmi, Tarun Khanna, and Ashutosh Varshney (2013) 'Caste and Entrepreneurship in India', *Economic & Political Weekly*, Vol. 48 (6): 52–60.

Jacobs, Norman (1971) *Modernization Without Development: Thailand as an Asian Case Study*, New York/Washington/London: Praeger

Jaffrelot, Christophe (2003) *India's Silent Revolution: The Rise of Low Castes in North Indian Politics*, Delhi: Permanent Black

Jodhka, Surinder S. (2002) 'Caste and Untouchability in Rural Punjab', *Economic and Political Weekly*, Vol. 37 (19): 1813–23

Jodhka, Surinder S. (2010) 'Dalits in Business: Self-employed Scheduled Castes in North-West India', *Economic and Political Weekly*, Vol. 45: 41–8

Jodhka, Surinder S. (2012) *Caste: Oxford India Short Introductions*, New Delhi: Oxford University Press

Jodhka, Surinder S. (2015) *Caste in Contemporary India*, New Delhi: Routledge

Jodhka, Surinder S. (2016) 'Ascriptive Hierarchies: Caste and Its Reproduction in Contemporary India', *Current Sociology*, Vol. 64 (2): 228–43

Jodhka, Surinder S. and Katherine Newman (2007) 'In the Name of Globalisation: Meritocracy, Productivity and the Hidden Language of Caste', *Economic and Political Weekly*, Vol. 42: 4125–32

Jodhka, Surinder S. and Aseem Prakash (2016) *The Indian Middle Class*, New Delhi: Oxford University Press

Kapur, Devesh, Chandra Bhan Prasad, Lant Pritchett, and D. Shyam Babu (2010) 'Rethinking Inequality: Dalits in Uttar Pradesh in the Market Reform Era', *Economic and Political Weekly*, Vol. 45 (35): 39–49

Keller, Suzanne (1963) *Beyond the Ruling Class*, New York: Random House

Khouangvichit, Damdouane (2010) *Socio-Economic Transformation and Gender Relations in Lao PDR*, Umea: Umea Universitet

Kremmer, Christopher (1997) *Stalking the Elephant Kings: In Search of Laos*, St. Leonards: Allen & Unwin

Kühn, Thomas and Jessé Souza (eds.) (2006) *Das Moderne Brasilien*, Wiesbaden: VS

Kumar, S., Anthony Heath, and Oliver Heath (2002) 'Determinants of Social Mobility in India', *Economic and Political Weekly*, Vol. 37 (29): 2983–7

Kuznets, Simon (1955) 'Economic Growth and Income Inequality', *The American Economic Review*, Vol. 45 (1): 1–28

Lahire, Bernard (1998) *L'homme pluriel*, Paris: Armand Colin

Landry, Bart and Kris Marsh (2011) 'The Evolution of the New Black Middle Class', *Annual Review of Sociology*, Vol. 37: 373–94

Lange-Vester, Andrea and Christel Teiwes-Kügler (2013) 'Das Konzept der Habitushermeneutik in der Milieuforschung', in Alexander Lenger, Christian Schneickert, and Florian Schumacher (eds.) *Pierre Bourdieus Konzeption des Habitus: Grundlagen, Zugänge, Forschungsperspektiven*, Wiesbaden: VS: 149–74

Lao Women's Union (GRID Centre) (2000) *Marriage and Family in the Lao P.D.R.*, Vientiane (typescript)

Leach, Edmund R. (1970; third edition) *Political Systems of Highland Burma*, London: Athlone Press

Locke, John (1967) *Two Treatises on Government*, London: Cambridge University Press

Luhmann, Niklas (1995) 'Kausalität im Süden', *Soziale Systeme*, Vol. 1: 7–28

Mallick, Ross (1997) 'Affirmative Action and Elite Formation: An Untouchable Family History', *Ethnohistory*, Vol. 44: 345–74

Marx, Karl (1953) *Das Kapital* (3 volumes), Berlin: Dietz

Marx, Karl and Friedrich Engels (1964) *Das Kommunistische Manifest*, Werke 4, Berlin: Dietz: 459–93

Massey, Doreen (1984) *Spatial Divisions of Labour*, London/Basingstoke: Macmillan

McLeod, William H. (2000) *Exploring Sikhism: Aspects of Sikh Identity, Culture and Thought*, Delhi: Oxford University Press

Mendelsohn, Oliver (1993) 'The Transformation of Authority in Rural India', *Modern Asian Studies*, 27 (4): 805–42

Merleau-Ponty, Maurice (1964) *Le visible et l'invisible*, Paris: Gallimard

National Statistical Center of Laos (2006) *Basic Statistics of the Lao P.D.R. 2005*, Vientiane: State Press

Naudet, Jules (2014) 'Finding One's Place Among the Elite: How Dalits Experiencing Sharp Upward Social Mobility Adjust to Their New Social Status', in Clarinda Still (ed.) *Dalits in Neoliberal India: Mobility or Marganilization?* New Delhi: Routledge: 236–58

Nederveen Pieterse, Jan and Boike Rehbein (eds.) (2008) *Emerging Futures*, special issue *Futures*, Vol. 40 (8)

Neri, Marcelo (2012) *A nova classe média*, São Paulo: Saraiva

Ngaosyvathn, Mayoury (1995) *Lao Women Yesterday and Today*, Vientiane: State Press

Nohl, Arnd-Michael, Karin Schittenhelm, Oliver Schmidtke, and Anja Weiß (2014) *Work in Transition: Cultural Capital and Highly Skilled Migrants' Passages Into the Labour Market*, Toronto: University of Toronto Press

Oesch, Daniel (2006) *Redrawing the Class Map*, Basingstoke: Palgrave Macmillan

Omvedt, Gail (1976) *Cultural Revolt in a Colonial Society*, New Delhi: Scientific Socialist Education Trust

Omvedt, Gail (2008) *Seeking Begumpura: The Social Vision of Anticaste Intellectuals*, New Delhi: Navayana

Pai, Sudha (2002) *Dalit Assertion and the Unfinished Democratic Revolution: The Bahujan Samaj Party in Uttar Pradesh*, New Delhi: Sage

Pandian, M.S.S. (1997) *Brahmin and Non-Brahmin: Genealogies of the Tamil Political Present*, Ranikhet: Permanent Black

Phomvihane, Kaysone (1985) *Niphon Leuak Fen* [Selected Papers], Volume I, Vientiane: State Press

Piketty, Thomas (2014) *Capital in the Twenty-first Century*, Cambridge, MA: Harvard University Press

Pochmann, Márcio (2012) *Nova classe média? O trabalho na base da pirâmide social brasileira*, São Paulo: Boitempo

Potter, Jack M. (1976) *Thai Peasant Social Structure*, Chicago: University of Chicago Press

Prakash, Aseem (2015) *Dalit Capital: State, Markets and Civil Society in Urban India*, New Delhi: Routledge

Raendchen, Jana and Oliver Raendchen (1998) 'Present State, Problems and Purpose of Baan-müang Studies', *Tai Culture*, Vol. III (2): 5–11

Ram, Nandu (1988) *The Mobile Scheduled Castes: Rise of a New Middle Class*, New Delhi: Hindustan Publishing Corporation

Rehbein, Boike (2007) *Globalization, Culture and Society in Laos*, London/New York: Routledge

Rehbein, Boike (ed.) (2011) *Globalization and Inequality in Emerging Societies*, Basingstoke: Palgrave Macmillan

Rehbein, Boike (2015) *Kaleidoscopic Dialectic*, London/New York: Routledge

Rehbein, Boike (2017) *Society in Contemporary Laos: Capitalism, Habitus and Belief*, London/New York: Routledge

Rehbein, Boike and Jessé Souza (2014) *Ungleichheit in kapitalistischen Gesellschaften*, Weinheim: Beltz Juventa

Rehbein, Boike, Benjamin Baumann, Lucia Costa, Simin Fadaee, Michael Kleinod, Thomas Kühn, Fabrício Maciel, Karina Maldonado, Janina Myrczik, Christian Schneickert, Eva Schwark, Andrea Silva, Emanuelle Silva, Ilka Sommer and Ricardo Visser (2015) *Reproduktion Sozialer Ungleichheit in Deutschland*, Constance: UVK

Savage, Mike (2015) *Social Class in the 21st Century*, London: Pelican

Schumpeter, Joseph (1955) *Imperialism, Social Classes*, New York: Meridian Books

Scott, James C. (1976) *The Moral Economy of the Peasant*, New Haven/London: Yale University Press

Singh, Pashaura and Louis E. Fenech (eds.) (2014) *The Oxford Handbook of Sikh Studies*, New York: Oxford University Press

Sisouphanthong, Bountavy and Christian Taillard (2000) *Atlas of Laos*, Chiang Mai: Silkworm

Smith, Adam (1998) *An Inquiry Into the Nature and Causes of the Wealth of Nations*, Oxford: Oxford University Press

Sommer, Ilka (2015) *Die Gewalt kollektiven Besserwissens*, Bielefeld: Transcript

Souza, Jessé (2007) *Die Naturalisierung sozialer Ungleichheit*, Wiesbaden: VS

Souza, Jessé (2009) *A ralé brasileira*, Belo Horizonte: Editora UFMG

Souza, Jessé (2010) *Os batalhadores brasileiros. Nova classe média ou nova classe trabalhadora?* Belo Horizonte: UFMG

Sridharan, Eswaran (2008) *The Political Economy of the Middle Classes in Liberalising India*, Singapore: Institute of South Asian Studies

Srinivas, M.N. (1955) 'Village Studies and Their Significance', *Eastern Anthropologist*, Vol. 8: 215–58

Srinivas, M.N. (1962) *Caste in Modern India and Other Essays*, Bombay: Media Promoter and Publishers

Srinivas, M.N. (2003) 'An Obituary on Caste as a System', *Economic and Political Weekly*, Vol. 38 (5): 455–9

Stierli, Markus, Anthony Shorrocks, Jim Davies, Rodrigo Lluberas, and Antonios Koutsoukis (2015) *Global Wealth Report 2015*, Zurich: Crédit Suisse

Stoll, Florian (2012) *Leben im Moment? Soziale Milieus in Brasilien und ihr Umgang mit Zeit*, Frankfurt/New York: Campus

Stuart-Fox, Martin (1997) *A History of Laos*, Cambridge/New York/Melbourne: Cambridge University Press

Swartz, David (1997): *Culture and Power: The Sociology of Pierre Bourdieu*, Chicago: University of Chicago Press

Taylor, Charles (1989) *Sources of the Self: The Making of Modern Identity*, Cambridge, MA: Harvard University Press

Terwiel, Barend J. (1975) *Monks and Magic*, Lund/London: NIAS

Thompson, Edward P. (1963) *The Making of the English Working Class*, Harmondsworth: Penguin Books

Thorat, Sukhadeo and Katherine Newman (2010) 'Economic Discrimination, Concept, Consequences, and Remedies', in Sukhadeo Thorat and Katherine S. Newman (eds.) *Blocked by Caste: Economic Discrimination in Modern India*, New Delhi: Oxford University Press: 1–34

Thorner, Alice (1982) 'Semi-Feudalism or Capitalism? Contemporary Debate on Classes and Modes of Production in India', *Economic and Political Weekly*, Vol. 17 (49–51): 993–9; 2061–86

Thorner, Daniel (1956) *Agrarian Prospect in India*, Delhi: Oxford University Press

Thorner, Daniel (1969) 'Capitalist Farming in India', *Economic and Political Weekly*, Vol. 4 (52): 211–12

Vaid, Divya and Anthony Heath (2010) 'Unequal Opportunities: Class, Caste and Social Mobility', *Proceedings of the British Academy*, 159: 129–64

Vester, Michael, Peter von Oertzen, Heiko Gerling, Thomas Hermann, and Dagmar Müller (2001; second edition) *Soziale Milieus im gesellschaftlichen Strukturwandel*, Frankfurt: Suhrkamp

Vitali, Stefania, James B. Glattfelder, and Stefano Battiston (2011) *The Network of Global Corporate Control*, Zurich: ETH (arxiv.org)

Weber, Max (1972; fifth edition) *Wirtschaft und Gesellschaft*, Tübingen: J.C.B. Mohr

Weber, Max (2011) *Die protestantische Sekten und der Geist des Kapitalismus*, Munich: C.H. Beck

Weiß, Anja (2017) *Soziologie globaler Ungleichheiten*, Frankfurt: Suhrkamp

Wittgenstein, Ludwig (1984) *Philosophische Untersuchungen*, Werke 1, Frankfurt: Suhrkamp

Wittgenstein, Ludwig (1989) *Vortrag über Ethik und andere Schriften*, Frankfurt: Suhrkamp

Zago, Marcel (1972) *Rites et Cérémonies en Milieu Bouddhiste Lao*, Rome: Universitas Gregoriana

Index